PRETZEL, HOUDINI & OLIVE

PRETZEL, HOUDINI & OLIVE

essays on the dogs of my life

Deborah Thompson

2018
Red Hen Press
Nonfiction
Award

Red Hen Press | *Pasadena, CA*

Book layout by Collin Spinney

Library of Congress Cataloging-in-Publication Data

Names: Thompson, Deborah, 1963– author.
Title: Pretzel, houdini & olive : essays on the dogs of my life / Deborah Thompson.
Description: Pasadena, CA : Red Hen Press, 2020.
Identifiers: LCCN 2020025812 (print) | LCCN 2020025813 (ebook) |
ISBN 9781597098564 (trade paperback) | ISBN 9781597098595 (epub)
Subjects: LCSH: Dog owners—United States—Biography.
Classification: LCC SF422.82.T47 A3 2020 (print) | LCC SF422.82.T47
  (ebook) | DDC 636.70092 [B]—dc23
LC record available at https://lccn.loc.gov/2020025812

Publication of this book has been made possible in part through the financial support of Nicole Foos.

The National Endowment for the Arts, the Los Angeles County Arts Commission, the Ahmanson Foundation, the Dwight Stuart Youth Fund, the Max Factor Family Foundation, the Pasadena Tournament of Roses Foundation, the Pasadena Arts & Culture Commission and the City of Pasadena Cultural Affairs Division, the City of Los Angeles Department of Cultural Affairs, the Audrey & Sydney Irmas Charitable Foundation, the Kinder Morgan Foundation, the Meta & George Rosenberg Foundation, the Albert and Elaine Borchard Foundation, the Adams Family Foundation, the Riordan Foundation, Amazon Literary Partnership, and the Mara W. Breech Foundation partially support Red Hen Press.

First Edition
Published by Red Hen Press
www.redhen.org

Acknowledgments

Thank you to so many. Thank you to brilliant poet and teacher Veronica Patterson, first of all, for starting me down this path. Thank you to all of the past and present members of the Slow Sand Writers' Society, especially Jeana Burton, Jerry Eckert, Teresa Funke, Jean Hanson, Luana Heikes, Sara Hoffman, Paul Miller, Karla Oceanak, Leslie Patterson, Sue Ring deRossett, Kay Rios, Elisa Sherman, Greta Skau, and Melinda Swensen. Thank you to the Department of English at Colorado State University for supporting my move from literature and literary criticism to creative nonfiction, and especially to my department chair Louann Reid and my colleagues Leslee Becker, John Calderazzo, Sue Ellen Campbell, Marnie Leonard, E.J. Levy, Steven Schwartz, and Sarah Sloane. Muchas gracias to Kelley Simpson for keeping me humble and, sometimes, sane.

Thank you to the following literary journals, their editors, and their staff, for improving and publishing previous versions of essays in this book: *Bellevue Literary Review*, vol. 16, no. 1: "Canine Cardiology," *Chattahoochee Review*, vol. 33, no. 2–3: "Scavenger Love," *Iowa Review*, vol. 40, no. 3: "Mishti Kukur," *Missouri Review*, vol. 38, no. 3: "As She Kissed the Cow," *Missouri Review*, vol. 32, no. 1: "What's the Matter With Houdini?," *Jabberwock Review*, vol. 38, no. 1: "Rescue Dogs," *Tattoo Highway*, no. 22: "Let Dog," *Wild Things: Domestic and Otherwise*, ed. Whitney Scott: "Heat," and *Xenith*: "Border Kali."

Thank you to the terrific team at Red Hen Press.

Thank you to all the dogs.

Thank you to Rajiv Bhadra, always.

Contents

1

Let Dog

My husband lies dying in the living room back home, while I roam the dog park with our three dogs, inhaling the meeting of mountains and plains in the foothills of Northern Colorado. To the west looms Horsetooth Mountain, and beyond that the great Rockies. To the east the prairies stretch to the horizon. You can see forever.

But dogs know only now, only here, only nostrils and panting and dirt.

The night before, the long night of May 31, our dogs kept watch, preternaturally still, while their human leader, my thirty-eight-year-old life partner, lay on the hospice-supplied bed, dying of liver failure caused by colon cancer. Rajiv had been in that somewhere-else state for over twenty-four hours: not unresponsive, exactly, but watching, looking with jaundice-dyed eyes at something beyond my scope. When he thrashed, I measured out an eyedropper of liquid morphine and massaged his throat into swallowing, as I'd learned to do with the dogs' oral medications. I gave myself tasks to hold together through the most important labor of our thirteen years together:

giving Rajiv the best death I could. When I changed his sweat-soaked T-shirt for a dry one—his arms obediently raising at my coaxing, though he didn't seem to recognize me—the dogs sniffed at the discarded wet shirt with dismay. I'd never before seen them work a scent with drooped, unwagging tails.

By the dark of morning, Rajiv stopped responding to my coaxing touch. I turned, exhausted, toward the sofa and the pull of needful sleep, but immediately he grabbed my arm and held tight, almost ferociously. Was this a new burst of life, or of dying? I lay on the edge of the narrow bed and held his once-cinnamon hand, now otherworldly golden. His arm curled around my waist, a move his body remembered how to do without his mind telling him. We lay that way all night, neither asleep nor awake, clutching together on the special bed, rhythmically inflating and deflating to prevent bedsores. Our dogs breathed with us to its hissing rhythms. Pretzel, our black mutt, devoted to Rajiv with Border collie intensity, slept at our feet, his crooked and underbitten jaw set stoically. Chappy and Houdini, fawn cocker mixes, my dogs more than Rajiv's, settled on the stairwell overlooking the bed, their spaniel noses open for a change in scent. We waited, all five of us, for light.

The night had been still and patient, but by the next morning Rajiv was pushing me away, throwing off clothes, turning his head aside fiercely when I tried to swab his mouth. Pretzel stirred restlessly on the bed with Rajiv's stirrings, rearranging his limbs without settling. Chappy and Houdini barked without direction, running from window to window to locate the source of their unrest. Did Rajiv know what was going on? Was he still there inside that reactive, bilirubin-soaked body? Was he in pain? Scared? How much longer would it be? Would I be able to hold out? I couldn't focus, couldn't structure my fears. For thirteen years I could endure any crisis with Rajiv by my side. I could even bear his death if I had his arms instinctively squeezing me. Without them, I couldn't. That's what they mean, I now understood, by *at a loss*.

By mid-morning, as Rajiv's throes subsided while mine accelerated, our doctor friend Kelley arrived to relieve me. *I can't live without Rajiv*, I told him, *I won't do it*. Kelley urged me to go to the dog park. When I protested, he commanded, *Go*, with Cesar Millan-like calm assertiveness. I submitted. He knew it was my sanctuary and sanatorium. It would rearrange my thinking, he said, and pull me out of the timeless nevermore and into the now.

The meaning of *now* is defined by the wagging of three tails—two bushy, one a stump—in response to the question, "Dog park?" Now shook uncontainably out of "stay" as I fastened collars. It unleashed, at the release command "okay," into staccato play-bows.

"Dog is my copilot," one bumper sticker blazoned to us as we pulled into the parking lot. Another car sported a "Praise Dog" sticker. Rajiv and I never fit in here in Protestant Fort Collins— nicknamed "Fort Caucasian." Raju, a Hindu agnostic to the end, and I, a devout Jewish-raised atheist, were regularly subjected to proselytizing and occasionally warned that we were going to hell. But in the dog park, evangelism was off-limits, except for the dog religion that we all half-jokingly practiced. One regular confessed to me that she thought that dogs were angels made flesh—and she meant this literally. She'd reached the danger zone of dogolatry toward which I was headed. When forced to hear or recite religious material that I didn't believe in, I mentally substituted "Dog" for "God": "In Dog we trust"; "One nation, under Dog"; "Let go and let Dog."

June 1 is a brazenly golden day. In the heat of noon, the dog park melts and spreads. None of the regulars are here, fortunately, so I don't have to talk to any humans in words. I walk around in a daze, checking my cell phone every ten seconds for missed messages from Kelley while the dogs scamper and scout, refreshing the inventory in their nostrils. I don't understand the sunlight. I don't understand the overwhelmingly blue sky, the striated clouds in mysterious pastel textures, far, far away and near enough to touch. The looming mountains to the west, the horizon to the east, I don't understand. They are too big, too beyond. The only reality is Rajiv dying in our living room on a bed that inflates and deflates with a sigh. When that ends, the world will end. Nothing else is real.

But dogs will not allow their reality to be denied. Once inside the fence, they do the noses-to-anuses circle dance, that dog-to-dog handshake, and then trot along the fence to check their pee-mail. Pretzel is already drooling. A misshapen, misbegotten, Dr. Seuss-like creature—his spaniel head too small for his leggy, Border collie body—he's got a crooked underbite that pushes his blackberry nose off-center. Kelley, who trained in pediatrics, told Rajiv and me that in the old days of medicine, when a child didn't look right, the doctor would note FLK (for "funny-looking kid") in the chart. So Rajiv and I called Pretzel an FLD. Now, after clenching his jaw all night, he finally relaxes it into a dog-smile.

The cockers, too, come back to life. Houdini, the cocker puppy, runs in three wide circles before plopping flirtatiously on a young woman's feet to be adored. Chappy lifts his sharp nose to divine a scent. Locating it, his triumphant tail flaps like wheat in the wind.

How can they live this moment in the dog park just exactly as they've always lived every other moment, for years? As if nothing else existed. As if oblivious to the obvious: that nothing will ever be the same again, that life itself will, in a few hours, stop being livable.

Now—as Pretzel dog-grins, as Chappy inhales, as Houdini scampers, as my husband lies dying—Allie, the grotesquely obese blue heeler, whose every snort bears the despair of a last breath, emerges from the shadows, crawls under my palm, and butts it for a petting. Her breath stinks, and she teeters dangerously. "She has heart and thyroid trouble," her owner apologizes to me. "There's nothing more we can do. She's not long for this world." But when I roll my palm along her scalp, her snorting—for just a second— stops. They say that petting a dog lowers not only the human's blood pressure and heart rate, but also the dog's. I feel my vitals lowering in the dog park. Kelley was right. When I quietly pet Allie, away from the ruckus of the other dogs, I can feel her vitals, too, calming under my hand.

As Allie leans harder against my palm, I stare at the dark spots on the white background of her heavy coat under the startling sun. In an instant they switch to white spots on a dark background. It's like the way the patterns of the black-and-white tiles in the bath-room used to shift for me when I was a little girl, when I learned how to stare hard and then let go. I step back, and the mountains become real, and then the endless stretch of prairie, and more real still is the big Colorado sky, where now meets eternity. The dogs and I are spots in an unreflecting landscape.

Back home, we found Rajiv awake and thirsty, though unable to swallow. But when I swabbed his dry lips, he closed them around the sponge end of the swab and sucked the water—hard. Kelley said that the sucking instinct is one of the first a baby presents, and one of the last a body lets go of. Rajiv was going back in time, back into his animal body, before language or loss. Late that afternoon, his mother arrived from India, barely in time to say goodbye. I turned the swabs over to her. She dipped swab after swab in water and fed them to Rajiv's sucking mouth.

At some point late in the night, while I was absorbed in the last rhythms of Rajiv's body, Pretzel jumped back onto the foot of the bed. Ma tried to push him off, but he kept returning, and I pled with her to let him stay. He curled into his pretzel figure, his rounded back touching Rajiv's ankle, his paws not overlapping pretzel-style as usual but pressed together as if in prayer. He lay in vigil at his master's feet until the last breath.

Years later, my dogs are still straining at their leashes to pull me back from nevermore. After a few days and weeks of mourning in their all-too-present ways—Houdini's explosive diarrhea, Chappy's refusal to leave my side, Pretzel's vomiting and taking refuge under the futon—the dogs quickly recovered their now. I took longer.

We're still dog park regulars. It's my second living room. The events of my life have been marked here. If I were a dog, I would still smell the markings: our strolling hand in hand, Rajiv and me, in shorts or in ski-jackets; my limping the perimeter through injuries and after surgeries; my walking with the dogs, outside myself, while Rajiv lay dying; my avoiding eye contact with other humans after his death; and eventually my dogs and I meeting a new generation of canine and human regulars, who had their own now, who knew nothing of our past.

I can still sense Rajiv's presence here, too, and the presence of his dying, the meeting of life and death in the panorama of mountains, prairies, and endless skies. Amid the dust and the dogshit,

I smell the ashes of his now. I touch it when I bend to pet the arthritic, slowly dying Allie, still miraculously alive all these years later, heaving and wheezing and snorting obesely as she stares at me through cataract-clouded eyes, not long for this world, as none of us are, but still taking joy in the dog park's smells and rhythms. I feel it in the hot snorts of her breath against my cheek when I kneel to meet her face.

2

What's the Matter
with Cocker Spaniels

"Houdini will eat himself to death," we'd say. The dog consumed pens, pencils, electric cords, bandages, pill bottles, photograph albums, even my treasured copy of *The Sexual Politics of Meat*, whose carcass he left strewn around the living room floor. Recently, as I pried a bit of freshly snatched gauze out of his gums, I remembered that it was the thirteenth anniversary of my father's fatal stroke. Why did that realization emerge along with the whiff of canine saliva? As Houdini made a second grab for the damp wad now cradled in my palm, the spittle-soaked dressing served as my American madeleine.

This is the story of how I—and, in a way, my country—became responsible for an inbred cocker spaniel with a death wish.

The last thing my father did before his stroke was to visit a pet store in the mall. I wonder if he already sensed the fatal clot dislodging and moving to his brain and if intimations of death impelled him toward new life.

Here's how I replay the scene: my mom, a fragile and graying Nancy Reagan figure and my dad, a sturdier Ronald Reagan build with the ex-president's flawless head of dark hair, walking hand in hand in the Parmatown Mall, rejoicing in the good news they'd just gotten from the cardiologist: the drugs were working, Dad's blood pressure was down, his arteries less constricted. His heart sounded good. At sixty-three years old, he was finally free to breathe. It seemed like an occasion to celebrate, and because he was now on retirement—a new enough state that he had to keep reminding himself it was so—my dad had the luxury of going to the mall on the way home so that he could pet some puppies.

Peering into the cages full of animals with expectant eyes, pink tongues, and downy fur, he chose the floppiest puppy of all, a cocker spaniel, the dog of his youth.

Soon after my father's death, my own dog pangs began. Something hormonal took over me, a thirty-three-year-old woman who'd never had any urge to procreate, so my partner and I got first a cocker-border collie mix, Pretzel; then Chaplin, a cocker-Pomeranian-poodle mix, both from the Humane Society. We were a happy family, we two humans, three cats, and two dogs. But in 2002 I bought a purebred cocker—and from a pet store, the worst sin.

My visit to the pet store, like my father's, occurred in death's vicinity. Rajiv, my life partner of thirteen years, had just finished his third ineffectual round of chemo for end-stage colon cancer. Doctors advised him to take regular walks in order to preserve his muscle mass, but it was too cold outdoors, especially since his latest chemo drug had made his skin hypersensitive to temperature, so we went to the mall, as my father had done six years earlier. Rajiv had begun calling himself "dead man walking," and did, in truth, walk like a B-movie zombie, his eyes failing to register the stimuli around him. In another week he'd be diagnosed with metastases in his spine.

The mall offered benches strategically placed every yard or so for the old folks to rest. Cancer had made us, at thirty-seven and thirty-eight, the old folks now. When we found ourselves at a bench outside Pet City, we had to go inside. A little cocker pranced and squirmed in his aquarium, just as Pretzel, now six years old and aging, must have done as a puppy. When Rajiv asked to hold the "little tyke," it was the first time in days that he'd expressed desire for anything, and when he held the puppy, he smiled for the first time in weeks. A few days later he went back and asked for the same puppy, the one with dumb curiosity and an endearing obsession to pull on our shoelaces. Again the Rajiv smile, the one I'd almost forgotten, the one spanning his whole face and stretching into his scalp, the one I'd do anything to bring back. So I purchased a puppy dumber than a hamster.

We bought our cocker as the breed's popularity was reaching its twilight. But when my father, a child of The Great Depression, owned the cocker of his youth, the breed was immensely popular. Ronald Earl Thompson, my father, had been born in 1931, in the small southern town of St. Augustine, Florida, to a white, lower-middle-class family, exactly the kind of family suited to adopt the emerging American Cocker Spaniel as a family pet, and for which the cocker would become a sort of mascot.

The American Cocker Spaniel split off from the English version of the breed as America was coming into its own. In 1936, American and English cockers were shown in the kennel club rings as separate breeds for the first time. In subsequent decades, America established itself as the upwardly mobile world power. During World War II, the dog appearing on twenty-five covers of the *Saturday Evening Post* was a playful black-and-white cocker named

Butch, based on illustrator Albert Staehle's own cocker spaniel. Sometimes he carried in his mouth a newspaper bearing war news, or he was caught in the act of an unauthorized panty raid, or seen with his head emerging from a broken lampshade, or some other materially destructive bit of naughtiness and was put in the dog house. But Butch's eyes were so pure and happy, his innocent brand of mischief so opposite the evil of the Nazis and the Axis forces, that he was instantly forgivable. As the good-hearted, defenseless underdog, this cocker was the face of the home front that America drew for itself. After the war, other cockers succeeded Butch as American cultural icons, from Spot of the Dick-and-Jane readers to Tramp's girlfriend Lady in the animated Disney film.

My father's childhood cocker was a new American classic, as playful as Butch and his successors. This was the cocker who kept my father company as he tended to his family's Victory garden. That "tending" included keeping the little cocker from digging up the vegetables, chasing the chickens, or chomping the pecans that fell from their majestic pecan tree. I wish I had asked my father what he'd named his dog, what games they played, what secrets he whispered into its dirt-mopping ear. As it is, all I know is that my father's first love was a cocker.

As he moved into his teen years, his blond hair darkening, and America into its post-war boom, the cocker gained even more in popularity. With the rise of cars and highways, middle-class whites moved out of inner cities, suburbs were born, and dogs became the family pet. Like the suburbs themselves, and like the lawns on which suburban dogs romped, cocker spaniels—the epitome of the family dog—gave us nature without the wildness; they substituted for nature itself a simulation of it, one that is dumb, loving, and submissive to its master. Cockers were the triumph of extended pre-pubescence for both dogs and humans, an achievement made possible by exploiting nature's plasticity.

All dogs are, in a sense, permanent puppies. A manmade species (or subspecies), dogs have no natural habitat outside the human realm. Some archaeologists believe that humans began breeding dogs from wolves somewhere between ten-thousand and thirty-thousand years ago by selectively keeping and reproducing the most submissive and sociable—that is to say, the most puppy-like—of wolf cubs.

But if all dogs are essentially wolf puppies, cockers are among the most puppy-like, the most inveterately and hopelessly immature. Bred centuries ago to flush woodcocks out of the forest undergrowth for hunters to shoot at and retrievers to return, cockers were selected for the puppy-like traits of inquisitiveness and distractibility, traits that made them pursue potential food without pause and follow every slight movement with exuberant curiosity. They were not bred to assess or deliberate, guard or guide, rescue or retrieve, but merely to stir things up and leave a ruckus for others to deal with. So it's no wonder that they have the curiosity and attention span of a human two-year-old.

They're also the dogs of American nostalgia. Patti Page sang to a cocker puppy in 1954 on The Morning Show, heralding in the era of the pet store, which quickly became a fixture in the emerging American strip malls. Puppies became commodities that one could window-shop for on a stroll. We learned to think of animals—and of nature in general—as plastic, malleable, and bendable to our ends.

During the time of the cocker's rise to popularity, my father also traveled a very American path. He was, in fact, almost a textbook

American success story. A bright kid, he took a special interest in science. As the synthetic polymers that had been developed during the World War II era—melamine, nylon, vinyl, polyester—were refined, commercialized, and mass-produced, and as pharmaceuticals and food additives proliferated, he was convinced that better living through chemistry was imminent and the future unlimited. Having worked in a pharmacy through high school for an avuncular pharmacist who encouraged him to go to college, my father did a five-year stint in the Air Force so that he could enter the University of Florida in 1954 on the GI Bill. He chose to major in chemistry just after Watson and Crick identified the make-up of the DNA strand, and graduated four years later, in 1958, with a young wife and a bachelor's degree in science. Convinced, like the family friend at Dustin Hoffman's graduation party in the 1967 film *The Graduate*, that there was "a great future in plastics," my father went on to get a PhD in Organic Chemistry. "Organic" chemistry was being redefined not as the chemistry of life but as the chemistry of carbon. He began his work as a research chemist in 1963 with a wife, two young kids (I joined the pack that year) and the American dream in tow. The newly minted Dr. Thompson went to work for Ferro Corporation on projects such as "polymeric hindered amine light stabilizers," "unsaturated ester group terminated polydienes as unsaturated polyester modifiers" and "multilayer thermoformable structures." For most of his career he tried to develop plastics that would last forever. Only in the last few years did he switch to plastics that could biodegrade.

The only item missing from the picket-fence dream my father created for his family was a family dog. Because my brother was allergic to dogs and cats, we grew up instead with a range of rodents and the odd reptile. My favorite photo from childhood shows my father urging a reticent hamster into my cupped hands. We shared many such moments. I kept mostly hamsters and gerbils—a string of them, as they died or escaped. I went through Frisky, Pesky, Fluffy, Freddy, Teddy, Piglet and, in college, Hamlet. My brother branched out into mice, rats, and rabbits, as well as turtles, snakes, and lizards. I don't think a single one of them died of old age. I learned the wrong way that rodents need water every day and that caged gerbils and hamsters will eat their young. I learned that when one pet died, it could be easily replaced from the endless supply at the pet store.

Had we gotten a family dog, it might well have been a cocker and almost surely would have come from a pet store, as all our other critters did. But the dark underside of pet stores was emerging as I grew from a kid in the 1960s into a teenager in the 1970s. Pet stores were a creation of the twentieth century, and with their emergence the dog became a domestic product. Cockers were particularly overbred. Before this, dogs would have been bought directly from breeders, who usually worked closely with their stock. But with the rise of postwar suburbs and suburban lifestyles, and as America began to think in economies of scale, puppies began to be mass-produced in "puppy farms" or "puppy mills." A better term might be "puppy factories" because at their worst these facilities treated, and still treat, dogs, particularly adult female dogs, as reproductive machines. Some of these dogs spend their entire adult lives pregnant or birthing, often stuck in cages stacked on top of each other, with little exercise or human contact. Even the possible satisfactions of motherhood are denied to them; the puppies are separated from the mothers as infants and shipped across the country to pet stores, which display them as if they magically appeared from scratch, as if no labor or loss went into their production. In the 1960s these puppies might be shipped to stores such as Sears Roebuck (which once sold pets) or to the emerging pet stores. Prospective owners would meet their puppies outside the context of parents or siblings or birthplace. A doggie in the window seems to come to its viewer as a fresh, new product without a past and certainly without a connection to a natural order.

In response, in part, to the rise of pet stores and puppy mills, as well as to animal cruelty on factory farms and in laboratories, the Animal Welfare Act passed in 1966, stipulating minimal acceptable standards for animal treatment, commerce, and research. Before the AWA, there were practically no limits on the kinds of surgical procedures and product testing performable on animals. Beagles emerged as the laboratory dog breed of choice. Some beagles got so many surgeries, often without anesthesia or even analgesics, that their skin had more scar tissue than fur. Animal ethicists have referred to these as "Frankendogs." These dogs must have endured unaccountable—and unaccounted-for—suffering.

The Animal Welfare Act was introduced in the 1960s of my childhood, an era when dogs came indoors, snuck onto the living room sofa, and nosed their way into the American family. No longer merely the hunters, workers, and guards they were bred to be, they gentrified into pets and companions and even family members. The primary impetus for the AWA was less the reduction of suffering of research animals and more the protection of people's family dogs against being stolen and sold to laboratories. This happened most famously to a Dalmatian named Pepper, who, according to the 1965 account of this dognapping in *Sports Illustrated*, ended up dying in the laboratory before his devastated human family could recover him. In fact, the act opens by acknowledging this motivation:

> Be it enacted by the Senate and House of Representatives of the United
> States of America in Congress assembled. That, in order to protect the
> owners of dogs and cats from theft of such pets, to prevent the sale or use
> of dogs and cats which have been stolen . . .

In 1966, following *Sports Illustrated*'s Pepper story, *Life Magazine*
ran an article titled "Concentration Camp for Dogs," which revealed gruesome laboratory conditions. The act continues:

> and to insure that certain animals intended for use in research facilities
> are provided humane care and treatment, it is essential to regulate the
> transportation, purchase, sale, housing, care, handling, and treatment
> of such animals by persons or organizations engaged in using them for
> research or experimental purposes or in transporting, buying, or selling
> them for such use.

After the Animal Welfare Act of 1966 (Public Law 89–544), life
got a little better for research dogs and "certain" other laboratory
species. Further improvements came with subsequent amendments
(see United States Code, Title 7, Sections 2131–2156).

The climate was changing. By the 1970s, following the publication of Rachel Carson's *Silent Spring* (1962) and Peter Singer's *Animal Liberation* (1975), environmentalism and animal rights had
emerged alongside the feminist, Black Power, and gay rights move-
ments. America was rediscovering nature as it disappeared and
expanding its notion of human rights to include the rights of the
nonhuman. Our past abuse of nature was coming home to roost in
such forms as cancer and carcinogens, environmental degradation
and loss of biodiversity. All I knew at the time was that cute cartoon owls told us, "Give a Hoot, Don't Pollute!"

Those were the idyllic days of my childhood, back when the

world was made for humans and particularly for Americans. To love nature was to consume it, and my father loved nature, as he loved his family and his country. Over the course of the 1970s he would shift from idealism and pride to defensiveness, as all his good work was being protested and he became labeled a corporate sellout and a polluter. As the 1970s rolled into the 1980s, chemical companies that produced pesticides, plastics, and pharmaceuticals went from being the hope of the future to the powerful forces of destruction in the American imagination. Though he never put it in these words, my father felt betrayed by the progressive forces of the country he thought he'd so faithfully served. As I shifted my own allegiances to environmental conservation, he took the generational shift in a deeply personal way. Even his own daughter went from idolizing him as the good father who stayed up all night rescuing an escaped hamster to condemning him as a patriarchal polluter. My father and I never had an outright confrontation or even animated discussion over our growing ideological differences. Perhaps we were guarding the love we still shared from the animosity scratching at the door.

As the environmental movement grew, so did the animal rights movement. Puppy mills and pet stores came under public scrutiny just as the cocker spaniel reached its peak of overbreeding. The inbred cockers of the 1970s took a nasty turn toward nervousness, irascibility, and fear-biting, along with a host of congenital health problems. When you try to control nature too tightly, we were learning, it bites back, just as the DDT-resistant mosquitoes were doing. We were learning that you can't just isolate one piece of nature and dominate it, that the world is one big ecosystem and every piece of nature is dynamically connected to other pieces. But by then it was too late for many species. The Endangered Species

Act passed in 1973, after the loss of hundreds if not thousands of identifiable species. It was also too late for that postwar American classic, the cocker. Americans treated the breed the way they do all things they no longer want—as disposable. The cocker currently ranks seventeenth among the most popular dog breeds in the US. Americans went on to embrace shepherds, beagles, Yorkies, golden retrievers, and especially Labrador retrievers as their new favorites and cultural mascots. The Lab is as iconic of early twenty-first-century America as the cocker was of mid-twentieth-century America (think of Bill Clinton's Buddy and of *Marley and Me*'s protagonist). But already the Lab, too, is showing some nasty signs of overbreeding and inbreeding.

I went on to share my life with an environmental engineer who did research first on anti-cancer drugs from rainforest plants, trying to find ways to produce the drugs without disturbing the rainforest, and then on clean-up of groundwater contamination by toxic waste from munitions factories. In essence, Rajiv's research was aimed at undoing all the damage that my father's generation of scientists and engineers did. But the drawback to working on anti-carcinogens is that they are carcinogenic, and working on cleaning up the TNT contaminating the groundwater means you have to work with TNT.

In 2001, after we had been together for twelve years, Rajiv was diagnosed with metastatic cancer, and as the year ended and 2002 began, there we were, buying a cocker at Pet City. My father came from an era of faith in stores and the market, an era when it was "natural" to modify nature for human consumption. But I should have known better.

We realized pretty quickly that Houdini wasn't quite right, but for a while his indiscretions were charming and kept Rajiv smiling through his chemo and radiation therapy. "Developmentally disabled," we joked, though really he was just dumb. But a particular kind of dumb. We erroneously named him Houdini after the brilliant escape artist, but our Houdini could get *into* just about anything, though *out of* nothing. He opened drawers and cabinet doors and devoured their contents, throwing up what wouldn't go through his short digestive tract, excreting whatever managed to make it through.

Houdini turned out to be not such a good dog for a dying man. Because he chewed everything, we needed to be on constant watch, which we couldn't manage. One day we got home from radiation to find toilet paper all over the house. Houdini had decided it was fun to grab the end of the roll in his mouth and run fast enough through the hallways to make the stream of toilet paper billow.

The next day we enrolled him in Canine Learning Center, where two evenings a week we were instructed on how to show Houdi who was master.

On a puppy school day in April, when Rajiv's radiation appointment was late, we brought Houdini to the waiting room. Rajiv's radiation oncologist was dog friendly, and Tracey, one of the techs, even kept a jar of dog treats at her desk for special visitors. When she came out to get Rajiv, I could see her melt and almost feel the maternal ache in her extended arms as I passed Houdini over to her for a cuddle. "Puppy breath," Rajiv concurred, watching Tracey inhale.

A greyhound emerged from a back room, followed by a patient. Because of the bald head and pink kerchief, I assumed she was being treated for breast cancer. Tracey lowered Houdini so that cocker and greyhound could sniff each other. "Where did you get your cocker?" the woman challenged. We told her. "No," she scolded, shaking her head. "No. You've supported a puppy mill. You're contributing to the suffering of thousands of dogs." She was loud enough to be heard down the hall.

"I know," I said sheepishly, "but . . ." I wanted to explain, but all I could think to say was that it didn't really matter because after Rajiv died, the whole world was going to end anyway. Just then the doctor popped out of his office, giggling to diffuse the tension. "I had a cocker once, growing up in Ecuador," he laughed. "But it got eaten by an ocelot. Man, that dog was dumb."

Rajiv laughed too, and the other patient strode off with her greyhound, well grounded in the world of the living. But Rajiv's footsteps as he padded to the radiation chamber were already otherworldly, unnaturally light and heavy at the same time, the tread of one so aged he's begun to lose his bearings, to disassociate from his body and its all-consuming pain.

Puppy school didn't go well. Every day now was presenting a new medical crisis for Rajiv, involving trips to doctors and testing labs and drugstores. We didn't do our puppy school homework and left the two older dogs, Pretzel and Chappy, to train Houdini as best they could. Pretzel was preoccupied with tending to Rajiv, but Chappy took his task seriously. With his sharp poodle nose, Chappy did his best to prod Houdini into some sort of order, some acknowledgement of the pack and its rules. But Houdini was so dense he left even Chappy baffled. On the last day of puppy school we got a bumper sticker declaring "My Dog is an Honors Student at Canine Learning Center," but we were way too ashamed of how Houdini had turned out to put it on our car.

In the darkest hour of June 2, four days after turning thirty-eight, Rajiv died at home, with his beloved Pretzel, along with his mother and me, at his side. Chappy stood at the top of the stairwell, on watch. Houdini, the dying man's bane, was upstairs confined to his crate, holding a conversation with himself.

When the hospice and funeral home workers came at three a.m., Pretzel jumped down from the bed and crawled under the futon, where he stayed for days. For weeks he couldn't eat, or, when he did, he threw up. His black face immediately sprouted white hairs, and soon, at six years old, his whole muzzle and eyebrows went white. I was too numb to mourn, but I felt grateful to Pretzel for taking on the role of my id and externalizing it for me.

Chappy assumed Pretzel's former role as my first mate and took that role very seriously. For weeks, sensing my vulnerability, he refused to leave my side, even at home. He mourned by serving and protecting.

Houdini remained Houdini, oblivious to the tragedy around him, happily snacking on the tissues that filled the wastebaskets.

Then came the "explosive diarrhea" (a term Rajiv's oncologist had used to describe a side effect of one of the chemotherapies), as if Houdini was mourning in his gut, leaving oozing fecal stains on the dining room floor. One evening, as I crawled on the carpet from spot to spot, crying into the piling and rubbing my knees raw as I wet-vacuumed, the smell as bad as the worst of Rajiv's ordeal, I decided I'd hit the lowest point of my life. The love of my life had just died and I was creeping among the feces of a disastrous cocker spaniel who wouldn't even let me grieve with dignity. Houdini tried to lick up the diarrhea while I competed with him to vacuum it up. Why couldn't Houdini be the one to die? I stared with hatred at his shit-encrusted face; he looked up into mine, then obligingly licked my nose. Hatred turned to disgust and then despair, and out of nowhere my numbness broke, as I sobbed into his putrid puppy fur, suddenly feeling fiercely maternal as I picked up the phone to call for a vet appointment.

It turned out that Houdini only had a "sensitive stomach," yet another common congenital ailment of the cocker. With special dog food, Houdi healed much more quickly and less expensively than the house did; that took hundreds of dollars and several visits by professional carpet cleaners.

I healed much more slowly, if "healing" is even what I did. Houdini, lacking memory or reason, for whom no past or future existed and only the present was real, kept me going. All three dogs made me get up every morning and leave the house at least once a day for a walk. Without them, I would have stayed in bed permanently. As the dogs regained their bearings, moving on to acceptance while I still lingered between denial and depression, they strained at their leashes to pull me into their now.

Years later, Houdini continued to shit rainbows. He ate right through pastel plastic bags—blue, green, yellow, translucent red—to get to the newspapers inside. Because dogs have much shorter intestines than humans, much of what he ate came out the other end undigested. There was no telling what I'd find in the backyard. I learned to keep plastic bags and newspapers out of reach, as well as pens and pencils and yogurt cartons and socks and underwear. But he managed regularly to snatch tissues and bits of paper and the stuffing from pillows; whatever he could, he ate.

Well into his adulthood, Houdini still had to be crated every night to keep him from eating himself to death while I slept. I learned this the hard way: one night I heard brittle crunching in my ear and woke up in time to dig the plastic of my three-hundred-dollar glasses out of the pockets of his gums. On the plus side,

Houdini would calmly submit to my prying fingers as I regularly dug everything from napkins to newspaper wads out of his esophagus. He barely noticed. If the item had gone really deep, he'd give a little aggravated cough before licking me and wagging his tail stump again. For him, my recovering items from his throat was a casual form of grooming.

Maybe I should have named him Peter Pan because of his inability to grow up. And maybe having a dog so endlessly needy, so permanently puppy, is what saved me at a time when I needed to be needed. Maybe I bought Houdini more for myself than for Rajiv in the first place, and maybe that's what Rajiv had in mind all along.

At the dog park, where Houdini jumped into laps or sat on feet and presented himself to be admired before rushing off to hump some attractive beagle or basset hound (perhaps I should have named him Casanova), people spoke dreamily about the cockers they had as kids—before enumerating the reasons why they would never get another cocker again.

Many of my friends, like the breast cancer patient at the radiation oncologist's office, looked on Houdini with disdain and on me with horror for his pet store origins. At the news of each new health problem, they rolled their eyes and said, "What do you expect from a purebred from a puppy mill?"

Sometimes I lied and said that Houdi, too, came from The Humane Society. Let this be my confession.

I also confess that I've loved Houdini for all the wrong reasons, the 1950s reasons, when we liked our nature cute and anthropomorphic. At the same time, I missed the natural wildness that must have remained in his DNA, dormant and unexpressed, the wildness I saw in Chappy when he pointed his sharp nose up like an antenna to catch an airborne scent or in Pretzel when he threw his head back and howled from the bottom of his lungs.

Much as I've loved my cocker, I, too, will never get another—or any purebred for that matter. My next dog, I vowed, would be a real dog, with pointed ears and nose. Maybe he'd even be able to express his own anal glands, something Houdini was too refined to do for himself. My next dog would be more than just a distraction from grief, more than a life-affirming mass of dumb, joyous love. He'd have some basic survival skills, too, and maybe some intelligence and independence and a hint of the lupine. Like Pretzel and Chappy, he'd come from a rescue shelter; I'm done with pet stores and puppy mills and manufactured adorableness.

As damaging as pet stores are, I'm glad my father was able to go to one right before his death. He would have had that look on his face as he held the ball of fur: an embarrassed tenderness hiding under mock sternness. Fingering the floppy, moth-wing ears, he would have looked into protean puppy-blue eyes over a licorice nose, while little white paws curled over each other around the sides of my father's hand like a pretzel. He would have smelled the puppy breath, with its hint of raw cookie dough. He would have felt the soft firmness of the tentative tongue, the flower-petal smoothness of the underbelly, the beating heart in his palm.

Five feet out of the pet store, my father stumbled. He must have been confused when he lost his footing, confused when he tried to ask for help but couldn't make words. My mother yelled to the security guard standing twenty feet away, and while he came running she focused on her husband's asymmetrically contorted face. "I think you're having a stroke," she said, fingering his frozen left cheek, looking into his cloudy blue eyes staring above his dumb mouth. Did he understand what was happening to him, what his wife was saying? Did he know, as he fell, where he was or where he was going? Could he still smell the scent of puppy breath lingering in his nostrils as he sank?

3

Among the Street Dogs
of Kolkata

In spite of the mange, I want to pet her. She's been lying in the powdery dirt road beside my mother-in-law's building in the Jodhpur Park area of Kolkata, India, but now she rises on her haunches as I move toward her. Distended nipples hang well below her ribcage, though there are no puppies in sight. The universal mutt, her ears neither stand nor droop. Her dull, short coat is brown or gray—or perhaps brindle, but this may be the effect of rivulets of dirt. Behind her every-dog face, her emaciated body hovers. Like homeless humans, this dog's age is undeterminable, but I'm guessing she's younger than she looks. She harbors an odor somewhere between stale urine and putrescence. I offer the back of my hand to her parched nose.

Keep your hands to yourself, Rajiv had warned me thirteen years earlier on my first of two trips to Kolkata, back when it was still Calcutta, when we'd first gone to visit his widowed mother soon after we got married. *Don't touch stair railings, don't touch the hands of beggars as you give them coins, and above all do not pet the street dogs. It is not sanitary.* Rajiv had grown up in India, and had only gone westward for graduate school, where we'd met. But I, a white woman who'd never been outside North America, was ungrounded by these Calcutta streets, where stalls spilled over onto sidewalks and everyone was squeezed together. When you're so close to the bodies around you, the barriers to touch matter more. And when there's so much dirt, cleanliness becomes a moral imperative. So on my first two visits I did as I was told: I didn't touch the street dogs. I looked at them with interest, pity, disgust, and longing, while they watched me with circumspection, alert for food or danger, neither trusting nor untrusting.

Not touching Rajiv was even harder. Back home in the States, whenever we felt the brush of the other's shoulder, we instinctively slotted our arms into a tongue-and-groove fit. Some portion of my skin was almost always in contact with some of his, even if it was just a finger scrolling down a neck, a thigh nudging a thigh, a palm molding itself around a love-handle. But here in India, Rajiv told me, men and women did not touch in public. It made the night-time touching, behind closed doors, all the more vital.

But now, on my third trip to India, Rajiv, as my mother-in-law puts it, "is no more." This time, I've returned alone to Kolkata to visit Ma, along with Rajiv's brother, Sujoy, and his wife, Joya, who are on an extended visit here for the summer. I'm still a privileged, first-world white woman, but I've been living in the liminal land of mourning, in the untouchable social space of widowhood. Grief, like culture shock, temporarily distorts the proportions of reality, skewing them into the cryptic streets of Kolkata, where nothing meets at right angles. Gradually you learn the new rules of reality and the new relations of your body to other bodies around you. Until then, grief is a trip to a third-world country. You don't belong in the privileged land of robust opulence, your home country, but where is home now? You can't find it even inside your own skin.

India would be hard for me, I knew, and India without Rajiv would be overwhelming. So I decided I'd do here what I did at home when I needed to fend off depression and anxiety: focus on the dogs. I now had three of my own—spoiled spaniel mixes who barked at paper bags, ate toilet paper off the roll, and couldn't even express their own anal glands. After Rajiv died, I'd counted on them to deliver reality in small, containable doses. Outside my house, too, I'd focus on dogs. Parties were bearable after his death only when a dog was in the house. Trips were kept from being impossibly lonely if I could find a dog to pet. When rolls of photos came back from the developer (in the days before the digital camera I got for this trip), half my pictures—I was surprised to find—featured dogs. Kolkata, I knew, would be full of dogs of all castes. I would keep my composure on this trip by studying them.

The hardest part of India would be facing my mother-in-law, whom I hadn't seen since those unreal days after Rajiv's death when, in one breath between moans, she'd thank me for my care of her son and then, in the next, tell me that if I'd fed him better, if I'd cooked fresh Indian food instead of letting him eat Chinese takeout during his last months, he might have lived. If I'd only had a hot meal waiting for him each evening of our thirteen years together, and monitored his eating better, as Joya did for Sujoy, he would never have developed colon cancer. If I'd insisted he spend less time at work and more time resting at home. If I'd given him children. If I'd been a more traditional wife. Hindered by her semi-deafness, my American accent, and the English I was confined to and which she couldn't lip-read, I don't know if Ma ever heard my attempts to defend myself.

"How is she?" I asked my brother-in-law when he picked me up from the airport, from which I'd emerged into some kind of night. We rode home though lampless streets.

Sujoy shrugged. "She never changes. India changes all around her, but always she is stuck in the past."

"Still crying all the time?"

"Crying, yelling. Brooding. Feeling sorry for herself. She wants to be pampered in her misery. Always she is wallowing, wallowing. She will try to entice you. You must not indulge her."

Ma's building was scaffolded with bamboo poles for renovations. Outside the steps I saw, through the late evening darkness, the contours of a sleeping dog, now rising from its side to observe us. For a moment its eyes caught the moonlight. Then it drooped its head back onto its front paws. I wanted to linger down there with the dog, but Sujoy was already loading my suitcases into the "lift."

Upstairs, Ma stood in the doorframe, wrapped in a white cotton sari, trying not to smile. Her face seemed sunken, though her skin was smoother than I would have expected for a seventy-year-old woman who'd lost both her husband and her son. I made to kneel but she pulled me up with an "Ah-ray!" (the all-purpose Indian rebuke), so I moved in to hug her four-foot-eleven frame. She smelled of incense and baby powder, but below her sari blouse, I could feel sweat on the exposed skin of her back, cool and sticky. When I pulled back, she smiled, and I could see that she'd lost most of her teeth. That's what her sunkenness was: her lips clutching toothless gums. Only three teeth still stood on the lower right side. Her smile lowered. "Why you have waited so long to come visit your Ma?"

I tried to apologize. "*Dhannobad.*" Then I realized I'd said thank you instead.

Ma ignored my failed Bengali. "Six years you have waited." She turned my face to the light. Her tongue rocked her three remaining teeth back and forth as she examined me. "Why you are looking so pulled down?"

I tried to laugh. "I *have* been on an airplane for nearly two days."

But Ma knew better. "You are looking so sickly-sickly. So many wrinkles you have gotten. You must use anti-wrinkle cream." A lightning-bolt crease formed between her eyes as she continued her inspection.

"Yes. I *must*." I failed to keep my sarcasm in check, knowing there were more imperatives to come. I *am* forty-five years old now, I reminded Ma. But I smiled to take the edge off my petulance, and felt my crow's feet form.

She hobbled over her osteoarthritic knee as she showed me the daybed I would sleep on and where I could hang my clothes.

"Ma," Sujoy said. "You are limping. We will call doctor about your knee."

"Ah-ray, what doctor," Ma answered.

"Yes, we will," Sujoy said. "And you must lose weight."

"I will go up soon enough," Ma muttered to me.

In bed, after all human sounds receded, I heard a semi-human, or perhaps sub-human, sound, like a swallowed sob coming back up. Then I heard it again, and again, until it transitioned into a bark, then a yowl. It was the call not of the wild, but of the street.

Where do the street dogs go in the rain, I wondered as I dissolved into the lumpy daybed and an anti-malarial medication haze. Though India was not yet into monsoon season proper, the rain came down hard that first night. Where is that mangy dog outside Ma's steps going to spend the night?

I woke up at 4:00 a.m. to the pouring rain, then drifted in and out of sentience as the rain gave way to shy bird chirps, then the brash caw of crows, and finally the bleats of street vendors. By 7:00 a.m. I rose to the window and looked past its art deco grates. Barefoot dark women wrapped in bright saris bent their heads under an already drenching sunlight. Men appeared in undershirts and more drab lungis or dhotis. Both carried large loads of food or raw materials—even planks of lumber—on their heads with casual balance. A metal collector clanked his cans as he called out for more. A man on a bicycle chanted, I assumed, the prices and attributes of the live chickens he carried upside down by their legs, five in each hand. And then the car horns began, horns that would sound all day long, ruining the magic.

My brother- and sister-in-law were gone by the time I brushed my teeth with bottled water, slipped into my salwar-kameez, and ventured into the common room. I poured more sterilized water into a coffee mug, popped it into the microwave, and then spooned my instant coffee into the steaming liquid. That was when Ma appeared in her billowing batik housedress, rocking from side to side to keep from bending her knees. I rose to hug her, but she stiffened. "Ah-ray! Still you are drinking coffee? You must not!"

"I know," I apologized, and sat back down.

"No. You must not."

Ma winced as I took a sip.

"So? They have left me," Ma stated.

"Left you?"

"Sujoy and Joya. Gone for entire day. They have things to do. They have no time for their Ma. Always they are criticizing, criticizing, I don't know what. I have my ways, they do not live here, they will leave me again." She rocked her three teeth with her tongue.

"They're only trying to help you," I said.

Ma turned a frown on me. "But Debby, you must not drink so much coffee. It is very bad for health. Do not drink."

I tried to think about dogs as I finished the coffee to keep Ma from killing my caffeine buzz. I was already sweating as I slipped into the kitchen to wash my mug, in spite of Ma's calling to me to leave it for the maid. "I'm going for a walk," I said, turning away.

"Ah-ray, in this heat!" Ma exclaimed. I closed the door on her muttering, "Always everybody is leaving me."

Outside Ma's apartment building, the mangy, crusty dog lies where I found her the night before. I extend my hand. But instead of bowing under my palm—the behavior offered by suburban US dogs—she cowers back. I expected feral—a lip-drawn snarl, maybe, or a low growl—but this dog is beyond docile, almost servile. She looks up at me from a lowered head. Her dirt-caked nose twitches as if trying to catch my scent, but she will not come closer.

Not petting dogs has always been agony for me, and I have indulged in every kind of human-canine flirtation to get a dog to accept my touch. But after Rajiv died, the need to touch fur, if not human skin, became almost mammalian, instinctual as a drive. Touch maintains your boundaries; it reminds you that you have an outline, a definition. The raw need for a defining touch, now denied, surprised me amidst my grief. Nobody, not even the grief support counselors, could have prepared me for this body hunger, the animal part of loss. Nobody warned me about the heavy emptiness of a chest no longer pressed, about the craving of skin suddenly deprived of touch, a dissolution that consumes the body like leprosy. It's not lust, exactly, or desire, or even longing; it's the way skin cries. Nobody talks about it, but widows know. Dogs know, too.

It's what makes suburban dogs leap onto chests and laps against all training. It's why street dogs might, in time, forego their instinct for survival to bow their heads into a human palm.

Does everyone, not just widows, have this need for touch? Does Ma? And if so, how does she live without its fulfillment, the skin always in wait?

I will work on this dog, I decide. I will get her to trust me. For now, I just sit with her.

Over the next few days I stand as close to her as she'll let me. I squat. Without more than glancing at her, I murmur, sometimes in English, sometimes in what little Bengali I know: *"Kee-ray. To-mee kamon acho?"* (Hey, you. How are you?)

I'd tried to learn Bengali when Rajiv was alive. He taught me words like *klontho* (tired) and *mishti* (sweet), and a few phrases like *ki kurchish?* (whatya doing?) and *ami tomai koop bhalobashi* (I love you very much) and *amar mishti pode* (my sweet ass). But mostly Rajiv got impatient when I tried to practice Bengali, and switched to English. My Bengali acquisition stagnated at the level of basic dog training, as I mostly just practiced on my three dogs, whom I called, alternately, *bhalo kukur!* (good dog) and *bajay kukur!* (bad dog). A common cry at the dinner table was *"bas!"* (enough) when, true to their spaniel natures, they hounded us for food. After Rajiv died, after the dogs mourned in dog-time and then bounded back to life just as my own mourning became real, I continued to speak Bengali to them. I even tried to get tutored by a native speaker, but when she taught me the alphabet, the fifty-odd characters all looked the same, and my hand fumbled like a kindergartner's trying to form letters I couldn't recognize. So when conversations among my in-laws now switch to Bengali, I understand how my dogs at home must feel all the time: trying to read body language, looking for a decodable sign amidst the general meaninglessness.

I take to calling this dog *Mishti Kukur* (Sweet Dog), careful not to accidentally slip into a similar term of endearment Rajiv and I regularly used for each other, "*Mishti Pode*" (Sweet Ass). The dog, cautiously, tolerates my presence.

"India is so spiritual," my American friends say. But they don't know my in-laws. Even Rajiv, around his mother, regressed to an ill-tempered, foot-stomping child as they vied for dominance.

"What you have done with my plates?" Ma asks Sujoy one morning as we finish breakfast. "The ones with the sky blue petals?"

Sujoy rises to the accusation. "Gone." He dramatizes with a sweep of his hand.

"Ah-ray?"

"We have thrown them out, Ma. We have gifted you new plates."

"We?" Joya shouts from the bedroom. "Leave me out of it."

"But I prefer my old plates for every day." Ma smiles defensively with flat lips.

"No. They all have chips and cracks in them. It is not sanitary."

"Ah-ray, not sanitary? I have used these plates for years. It is my home."

"It is not sanitary," Joya calls, concurring with her husband. "Germs can grow in the cracks."

"You hoard and hoard," Sujoy accuses her, emboldened. "We have gifted you such nice new items, but you refuse to replace. It is insulting. Yes, I would say that. It is insulting."

Ma looks to me for support, but I turn away. "What insulting?" she offers on her own. "I am an old lady on a pension. I must save. After six weeks you will leave. I am still here."

"Yes, I will leave. I will leave. Why should I stay?"

"Other widowed ladies live with their sons. I am all alone. But I will go up soon enough."

"Here we go." Sujoy throws up his hands.

"Rajiv did not treat me this way. So much disrespect you have for me. Rajiv—"

And now Sujoy is yelling in Bengali, and Ma is yelling back. I can't understand the words anymore, only the rising voices. They turn to me from time to time for affirmation, Ma especially, forgetting that I can't understand. Trying to read body language, I feel like my dogs at home, looking for a decodable sign amidst the general meaninglessness. I perk up when I can pick out a few Bengali words, just as my dogs liven with the recognition of "treat" or "walk" or "toy." But mostly I go into rest mode, mentally stretching my chin out flat against the ground, as my dogs would do when Rajiv and I argued. On those rare times that Rajiv and I fought, though, Pretzel used to flee under the dining-room table until it was over. I decide to follow his example. As I pass by Joya's bedroom, she mutters, "So much botheration all the time."

I stretch out on my daybed in the guestroom with *Travelers' Tales: India*, the book I've been reading when I'm feeling particularly foreign. One writer says that for some Western sojourners, INDIA comes to stand for I'm Not Doing It Again or I'll Never Do It Again. When the fighting flares up, I vow to myself that I'll never return to India, except possibly for Ma's funeral.

Photographs of Rajiv are all over Ma's flat. Formal portraits, graduation pictures, vacation photos. He joins pictures of his father in a collage of the dead. Sujoy and Joya (of whom there are far fewer pictures displayed) criticize this shrine, saying that Ma willfully dwells in death and morbidly refuses to look to life. That she's devoted her life to committing daily metaphorical *sati*. "You live only in the past," they scold her. "You refuse to move on. Life must go on." But they don't know widowhood and loss. They only think they do.

I like Ma's display. I'm glad to see that someone still acknowledges Rajiv's absence. The rest of India has forgotten. The relatives who come over don't refer to him. They ask me how I am "keeping," and note that I am looking "pulled down." But there's no mention of the heaviness of loss that's pulling me down. It's as if Rajiv never existed, or as if his nonexistence is unspeakable. Ma's display stands in passive-aggressive defiance.

But I don't step up to defend Ma or her shrine. Instead, at times like these, when I despair that the family is a kind of broken that can never be fixed, I resort to pulling out the photos of my Colorado dogs that I brought as part of my sanity pack. My father, before his stroke, used to be able to lower his blood pressure by imagining himself petting a golden retriever. I dream of spaniel fur.

"What are these?" Ma asks, catching me with my photos one day. "You must display."

She places my loose snapshots of Pretzel, Chappy, and Houdini around the house among the framed photos of Rajiv. She understands. We stand side by side, leaning in to look together at my spaniels. Our bare shoulders brush. Then I feel Ma pull back.

"And where are your photos of Raju? You do not travel with pictures of him? Only your dogs is it?"

Outside, the street dogs have receded into the shadows. I look for Mishti Kukur, but see no sign of her. It's so hot that even the dingy concrete buildings burn white. As I stride into the more commercial districts with their shops and stalls, I find more street life, if not liveliness, and a bit more English, at least on street signs. The vendors, shoppers, and laborers all move in measured steps. There's a certain kind of Kolkata walk, I've noticed, as if the dampness weighs everyone down. I'd congratulated myself on my first-world, well-cared-for body, but now, I notice, I'm gradually adopting this walk too, though not soon enough. Within two miles, I'm exhausted. Beyond hot and tired, I'm nauseated, and my gym-built leg muscles are cramping. I need to learn how to move with the heat rather than defy it.

The dogs have this walk too. Dogs don't run here. At most, they trot. But more often they slink, slouched, heads bowed to the sun. "There are no puppies here," I think. Not only have I not seen a single puppy, but I've seen no dog-play, no boisterous lumbering or bounding or scrapping to relay the sheer joy of having a body.

Lunchtime hits all at once. Tiffin-boxes appear as people sit along roadsides in bits of shade and heat tins of food over low flames. The workers fill their plates with rice and just enough gravy to hold the grains together as they mold balls with their fingertips. I think of the small pat of rice I take with meals to support a ladleful of curry and realize how greedy I've been. The pace of street labor lowers as men and women alike squat over their food. Then I notice the dogs, hovering and watching the slow, steady eating of humans. My three dogs would be leaping onto laps, diving into plates; I often have to fend them off with out-thrust elbows as I try to carry a forkful to my lips. But these street dogs are calm, waiting, civil, almost as if trained.

When the eating is done and I can smell the post-meal puja incense, the dogs creep forward. Each seems to know whom to go to. Casually, humans drop leftover rice or mango peel or fish bones to their waiting dogs. Each human seems to have a different click or caw for his dog. The dogs bow gratefully into their food. I watch a cluster of three dogs, one black and two mutt-brown, feed in order of hierarchy, the black dog first.

Rajiv would have been able to tell me more about these interactions: Do the same people feed the same dogs every day? Do they give the dogs names? Do they "own" them? Or maybe the humans don't own the dogs, or the dogs the humans. Maybe there is just a kind of belonging.

Does my Mishti Kukur belong to anyone? Does anyone feed her?

As the three dogs take their last licks, two spots of white appear down the road, whiter than any white I'd seen in Kolkata, where even the pages of new books seem to wilt and yellow overnight. These whitest white spots turn into two fluffy Chihuahua-sized dogs being walked on leashes by an Indian man in a polo shirt, flat-front pants, and Bata sandals.

"Papillons?" I ask the man, stopping him in his tracks.

"Ah, you recognize? You are the first to guess correctly. Most people say Chihuahua."

"I noticed the butterfly ears." It feels strange to speak in easy English. "They're beautiful."

"My wife's. Purebred."

The little dogs yap, and when I squat to pet them, their tails quiver. "May I?"

"Absolutely you may."

Their fur feels so soft in my fingers I could cry. How these little dogs tolerate such long fur in a place like Kolkata I can't imagine. They must get bathed often, and brushed every day. As I pet the Papillons, even letting them lick my face, the three street mutts approach from behind, and sniff the butts of the purebreds, smelling the residue of privilege. But as I move to shift my hand onto the black dog's dusty head, the man shouts "*Chup*!" and mimics a karate-chop to scare off the strays. Then with a "*Challo*!" he and his unnaturally white Papillons trot quickly on.

I'm beginning to identify the caste system among India's dogs, even as the country is trying to eliminate it among its humans. These two Papillons are *brahmins*. I've also seen a few *ksatriya* or perhaps *shudra* service, police, and search-and-rescue dogs. There are also the *vaishya* and *shudra* rural working dogs who guard, protect, hunt, and herd, and who, like their human counterparts, tend to be strong and lean, hungry-looking but not starving. Vastly more numerous, though, are these *dalit* dogs of the streets, literally untouchable with their mange and ticks and oozing wounds.

I walk through Kolkata's residential and commercial streets with my camera, documenting the class system of dogs, until I'm sick with heat exhaustion and dehydration.

On my way home, evening emerges in lengthening shadows. Rounding a corner, I come upon three tan dogs. Two, though mangy, are perched regally on a sand pile, as if posing for a photo. I take it. The third, who seems to have a touch of beagle in him, digs into the dirt to unearth a cool spot, then plops his belly onto it. This digging gesture contains more dogness—what I recognize as dogness—than I've seen yet in Kolkata, and I'm touched. I take his picture too, and capture his jaw relaxed into a grin. But when I step closer into their territory, one lets out a serious bark. It's the opposite of the yipping my dogs emit at my front door when the bell rings; those sounds are all energy and anxiety and excitement. This bark is calm, directed, purposeful, and efficient. I have no doubt what it means: *Do not come any nearer. Do not touch*.

I don't.

On the next block a blue heeler mix steps towards me, but as I try for his picture he trots past. "Ah-Ah!" I hear behind me, and the dog turns as I do to observe a man's hand gesture. The dog stands still for me to take the picture. Poor thing has yellow pus coming out of his eyes, and scabs across his thinning back. The man, skinny in his T-shirt and lungi, looks over my shoulder to see the dog in the viewfinder, then does the sideways head wag with a touch of pride and lets forth a string of Bengali, which I try to tell him I don't understand, but he only speaks louder. I smile and nod and mumble "*Jani na*" (I don't know), as Ma often does to me. Then, pointing to the dog, I ask, "Name? *Nam kee?*" But the man doesn't understand my attempt at Bengali and makes his apologetic side-to-side head gestures when I try again. I want to ask the man if the dog is his but don't have the language. So I point to the dog, then him, then raise my eyebrows into questions. He's puzzled. Dog-you, I point, dog-you. "Ah-cha-cha," he nods. I don't know quite how my question has translated. Does he understand himself as owning the dog? Or is there simply a link between them, a hyphen, the line my finger draws from dog to man?

When I stumble back home, Mishti Kukur is waiting. I hold out my hand, and she makes to sniff it, but I can't hold back any more, and as I rush to pet her, she pulls back, as if offended at my brashness. I call and chant, but she will not come closer.

The next day I realize just how much I overdid it on my reckless walk through Kolkata in the mid-day heat. I'm so sick that I can't go out, can barely stand to wear clothes, and take refuge in one of Ma's housedresses. I'm even walking like her now, slumped in her batik moo-moo as if weighted down by a dowager's hump. We sit together in front of the television watching Hindi serials while Ma narrates and explains the back-story intrigues. "This lady, she is very fond of this gentleman, but he does not know, and she cannot tell, because both are engaged to others. This lady here, she is an evil one, a double-cross. This gentleman, he is evil too, with mustache. You just see." She shakes her head disapprovingly as the music swells.

When the serials are over and the news comes on in alternating Bengali, Hindi, English, and Sanskrit, Ma hobbles to the fridge, her large belly teetering over crackling knees. She takes out a tiffin-box of gravy-soaked rice, rice she'd badgered me to finish eating at lunch when I couldn't eat any more, rice that Sujoy had yelled at Ma for storing instead of throwing out. Ma now scrapes the sticky grains onto a banana leaf. "Give this to your dog."

"My dog?"

"I see you from balcony. Poor thing must be hungry."

What else does Ma see?

"Don't tell Sujoy," she hastens. "He will go wild."

I squeeze her hand before taking the food out for Mishti Kukur. Inside this squeeze I feel the memory of another squeeze. In what would turn out to be the last few weeks of Rajiv's life, though none of us dared to think it at the time, Rajiv had taken to lying on the dining room floor with his feet up on a chair, to straighten the bones in his tumor-laden, radiated spine. His feet had become swollen from electrolyte imbalances and ached when he took off his compression socks. One day I walked in on Ma massaging Rajiv's feet in her lap as he lay below her chair, with Pretzel, our oldest dog, pressed against Rajiv's side. Ma murmured to her son as his moans lessened. Then, feeling watched, perhaps, she looked up, irrationally guilty when she saw my face, perhaps recognizing my irrational jealousy. Thirteen years of competing for Rajiv's love all concentrated into this moment as I fixed my eyes on Ma. Then she astounded me: she offered me Rajiv's feet. Wordlessly, she gave up her chair for me, positioned Rajiv's feet in my lap, and, as Pretzel repositioned himself, showed me how to squeeze in the right rhythm, her hands squeezing over mine. I had forgotten this moment until now, though I'd remembered all her scoldings.

I squeeze the banana leaf in memory as I carry it outside, where the sun has washed all life into the shade. I call out for Mishti Kukur, until I hear a rustle. She sticks her neck out from her little cove under the building, then tests a front paw. Her nose is working, registering the gravied rice, registering me. I walk away from the banana leaf and turn my back to show her I'm not claiming it. It's hers. She edged toward it, watching me intently without making eye contact. When she gets to the pile of rice, she pulls it, leaf and all, into her own private corner under the building overhang, and eats, watching me the whole time, as if she's confused because I've violated the social structure, as if she's so settled into her untouchable status that it's become instinctual to her. When she backs into the shade, I call to her for a while, but she doesn't come back out, just watches me peripherally through crust-lined eyes.

Sujoy and Joya are out all day long now, having given up on getting along with Ma. When they leave early in the morning, to visit friends and shop and run errands for Joya's parents, they tell Ma not to wait up for them at night. They take multiple Kinley water bottles and leave. But I've been spending more time with Ma, having lowered my caffeine intake and settled into her pace. We eat dinners alone at 9:00 p.m., when Ma gives up hope of their mealtime return.

"Why my own son cannot have dinner with his mother?" she asks one night, a few days before I am to leave. "Why is he so selfish? I tell you, Raju was not like that. Raju respected his Ma. He was not so childish."

"That's not entirely true," I offer. "Raju could be childish with you too, remember." But her deafness and her resolutely revisionist memory keep her from hearing me.

"He was a very loving boy, isn't it? Such a good boy, so loving. He never gave me any trouble."

"He loved you very much. But it's not fair to compare Raju and Sujoy."

"I have never!" Ma protests. "I do not do this thing, this compare. I have never. But I tell you, you say Raju he loved me, but Sujoy does not love me, I don't think so. But I will go up soon, and then . . ." She fills in the pause with a chin thrust as she sucks in her three teeth.

"Oh, I'm sure he loves you," I try again. "I'm sure of it. He just has a hard time expressing it. He gets frustrated. But he does love you."

"I do not think so," Ma says simply. She shakes her head, then sobs. "I don't know why God has been so selfish, so selfish. To take both my husband and my son. Both!"

I warm her hand in mine while she cries. She looks at me through layers of wet. "I know you are feeling pain, every day I am thinking about how you are all alone. But you have not given birth to him! You don't know what it is to lose him to whom you have given birth. Nine months and ten days I have carried." She floods again, but I withdraw my hand. I know she's right, that her suffering is bigger than mine, but I do not like "this compare." She fumbles for her handkerchief.

"I have been meaning to ask you." Ma snorts back down her rush of snot. "When he was dying, Raju, he kept clawing at his wrist. Just like this. I could not figure out what. Then I saw, and I took off his wristwatch, and he settled. What was that? I have been meaning to ask you all these years. Do you know what it means?"

I nod. "They call it the death throes. I didn't use to believe in it until Rajiv. It's a phase that dying people go through, where they sometimes grab at their clothes or try to throw everything off them."

"I don't know. What is it?"

"Death throes," I enunciate, separating the two words, but Ma just shakes her head.

"I don't know. He would not let me touch him. He threw off my hands. When I tried to hold him he shouted *Debby! Debby! Debby!* Thrice, just like that. You remember?"

I remember. His last words. But he did not settle after that. He struggled, fighting with his clothes, his caregivers, with death itself. The life-force was so strong in him, as it is in all of us, so recalcitrant and powerful even in death. Especially in death.

Later in that endless night of Rajiv's dying, after he'd lost speech and possibly cognition, he was awake and thirsty, though unable to swallow. But when I swabbed his dry lips, he closed them around the sponge end of the swab and sucked the water—hard. Then I'd realized that it was Ma's turn. I'd held out the swab to her, and she offered it to her baby son, as if in her own instinctual rhythm, dipping swab after swab in water and feeding them to Rajiv's sucking mouth.

"Do you remember the mouth swabs?" I ask her now.

"How he clung to life!" Ma is crying again, heaving, and when I offer her my arms she doesn't hesitate. When I first met my mother-in-law, and when I complained about her over the years, bristling at her free-flowing advice, it had never occurred to me that I would share the most absolute moment of my life with her, the moment when, as we each held a cold hand and Pretzel stirred at his feet, Rajiv gulped in a breath, then exhaled, then waited. We waited, too, for the next gulp. Instead, his face relaxed, the muscles completely at rest. Pretzel jumped down from the bed and crawled under the futon. Ma touched her hand to her son's cheek and said, with as much simplicity as wonder, "Absolutely cold."

Now my hands press into the fat of her back, pushing her ample breasts into my training-bra-sized ones. I can feel her lungs empty and expand.

Outside a street dog is crying. Not whimpering but crying in complete dogwails: Owww-owww. I wonder if it's my Mishti Kukur. Behind this lone voice, the car horns honk on.

It's finally time to hug Ma goodbye. My suitcases are already downstairs. I offer Ma my arms, but she stays fixed. "And so, Debby, you will go back to your dogs and forget all about your Ma." When I pull her into me, the hug triggers in her a convulsion of tears. I can feel it starting from her gut, pressed against mine. "I will go up soon," she cries. "I will go up and be forgotten. You will remember your Ma? You will not forget?"

"I will miss you, Ma," I say into her right ear, the less deaf one. "I love you."

I don't know if she understands the words, but she calms some and then pulls back to hold me by the elbows. "But Debby," she says, "you must not get any more dogs."

"You're right." I try to laugh it off, but already the word "must" is chasing away my tenderness. "I *must* not."

"No, you must not. It is too much. And also you must not let your dogs lick your face. It is unsanitary."

"Yes, Ma," I manage, approximating politeness. I know what

she's doing; she's trying to mother me in the only way she knows: to treat the ones she loves as children to be scolded. And that's what I become. Already I am determined, though the thought had not previously occurred to me, to get a fourth dog before the summer is out. And it won't be something cute and small and cuddly, like my three cocker mixes; it will be something muscular and lupine and vital, with a sharp nose and pointed ears and drive, something tough and third-worldly. A survivor.

Ma is sobbing now, in heaves. "Be strong," Sujoy rebukes, as he and I board the lift. I wave at Ma as Sujoy closes the black metal gates and we descend below her bowing bulk.

The driver that Sujoy hired waits for me at his car with my bags as I walk around the building, calling for Mishti Kukur one last time. I need to say goodbye. I've got something special for her in my pocket. When I put on my jeans this morning, the first time I wore them since my arrival in India, I discovered a bit of Snausage in the front pocket, left over from a trip to the dog park back in Colorado. It's stale, but still smells of artificial bacon flavor. I call at Mishti Kukur's cove, and her head emerges, bowed below her shoulders. Her nose is evaluating. She makes eye contact, drops her eyes immediately, but, when I encourage her, looks straight at me. I hold out the Snausage. Her jaw drops into a tentative smile, and she pads towards me with only an instant of hesitation, as if she recognizes and even trusts me. After I hold out the Snausage, and she takes it from my hand, she retreats two steps, but only two.

"I'm gonna miss you, Mishti," I say to her. "Will you miss me?" I hold out my hand for her to sniff. She keeps several inches between us, her nose so caked with dirt I don't know how any scent molecules can get through. Then I remember the water bottle holstered in my fanny pack. I cup some water into my hand and offer it to her.

She looks at it, then looks at me. I look away to show her I'm not interested, not threatening. She risks it, inches forward, stretches her pale tongue, takes a quick lap. Then another. I pour more water into my cupped left hand and, as she laps, slurping now, I set the water bottle down and touch her head with my right hand. Under my fingers, the dirt crunches as my pat turns into a stroke. *Wash your hands*, I imagine Rajiv's voice, joking and commanding. But this time I ignore it. My Mishti Kukur is starting to belong to me, and I to her.

And now I will abandon her. Will she remember me, look for me, wonder where I went? Will she find another human? Will she risk belonging again? From the car window, the first step of my long journey back to my very touchable dogs, I look at Mishti Kukur one last time. She's still waiting, watching me, as her small brown body recedes into the dirt.

We drive through streets and streets of dogs, myriads of un-touchable dogs, a country full, mixing, as the landscape shifts from urban to semi-rural, with the rib-lined goats and cows and chickens and people. I want to feed them all, even as they recede from my alien touch, even as I fly from Kolkata to Mumbai to London to Denver and the skins of travelers get whiter and whiter, even as I am greeted at my own front door by three anxious dogs—no, not dogs, but full-grown puppies, never to mature into real adults—who jump on me wildly. When Ma was last here, in those days after Rajiv's death, she scolded them for such behavior, pushing them away with an "*Ah-ray? Bahjay kukur!*" (Bad dog!) But she is not here, and I, instead, encourage my untamable first-world dogs to bark and croon and wiggle and shake under my greedy, fur-starved fingers.

4

Border Kali

Prayers, we'd always thought, were the worst kind of denial-ism, the primary repression of reality, but when Rajiv was di-agnosed with terminal colon cancer, we collected prayers from as many religions as possible—Christian denominations, Judaism, Hinduism, Islam, Buddhism—just in case one would "take." Even atheists sometimes long for miracles.

In better days, we made rationalism our ethic, and tried to merely laugh at magical thinking. As devotees of our three dogs, we'd replace the word "God" with its anagram. *Dog bless America*, we'd joke, or *My Dog is an awesome Dog*. Now we lived our Dog-gism, finding our only comfort in each other and our canines, who offered neither prayers nor hope, only *is* and *now*.

In the end Rajiv returned to the imagery of Hinduism, his mother tongue. It gave him comfort even without belief. I had rummaged through our stash of India souvenirs and found sev-eral large batik wall-hangings. Although I'd lived with Rajiv for twelve years and had been to India twice, I still didn't understand the Hindu pantheon, so I chose randomly. I hung up images of Ga-nesha, the elephant-headed god; of Vishnu, the younger and more serene of the Hindu trinity; and of Kali, the black and bloody warrior goddess adorned with severed human skulls. Rajiv chose to meditate cross-legged in front of Kali with our dog Pretzel nested in his lap. Rajiv was trying, he said, "to come to terms with my mortality." The metastases had by then so overtaken his liver that it bulged under his scaled ribcage. His cinnamon skin went so golden he glowed before Kali. What comfort had Rajiv found in this goddess of blood and skulls? Or was it something else that he found?

Two days after he turned thirty-eight, Rajiv's liver failed. Hospice workers set up a bed in the living room. To prevent bedsores, it inflated and deflated in alternating sighs. Kali stared down at his wasted body, while his Bengali mother bent over one side of the bed and I over the other, each holding a cold hand. Pretzel curled into a heart at his master's feet, while the younger two dogs cowered against the wall below Kali's effigy. At the funeral home, Ma and I each took an end of the gurney and shoved Rajiv's corpse into the incinerator's unearthly hot fire, so orange it burned red. The flames leapt hungrily into the frail body and instantly devoured it into their redness. When I returned home I took the batik images down. The gods were as worthless as prayers.

I thought I was done with Kali.

Even though Rajiv had been sick for eleven months, even though he'd been through four rounds of chemo, even though the liver metastases grew from CT scan to CT scan while the cancer blood markers went up in geometric progression, and even though he'd regularly been told by every doctor that he wouldn't live much longer, I went into shock after Rajiv died. The fact of his death was literally unacceptable to my consciousness. Reality melted into illusion.

While I was in shock, our three dogs, spaniel mixes, lived the trauma in their bodies. Pretzel took it hardest. When the hospice workers had arrived to remove the body, Pretzel crawled under the futon and, because dogs don't weep, vomited for three days. Widows of legend have turned white-haired overnight, but it was Pretzel who did this, not me. His muzzle went powdery against his black fur, and half-circle white eyebrows arced into umbrellas over his eyes. Houdini, the youngest dog, grieved in his guts and splattered loose stools all over the house. Chappy, the middle dog, always a mama's boy, became my protector, rarely leaving my side.

Eventually, all three dogs quietly overcame and "moved on." When we finally returned to our local dog park, Houdini ran in circles while Chappy monitored with exuberant officiousness, moving farther and farther from my side. Pretzel wandered the grounds in a dementia haze—as if he'd left something here, but couldn't remember what—between bouts of humping. Eternal puppies, they harbored no ancestral wolf, no instinct that death or danger lurked behind every tree. They bounced back into tennis ball innocence.

I knew I was supposed to follow our dogs as they pulled me, from the ends of their leashes, into their eternal present. But what about Rajiv's purple-calloused hands, which had combed their manes? What about his soccer ball-dribbling walk? What of the whiteness of his teeth against his brown-rimmed smile, ready to savor each delicious irony? Neither atheism nor Doggism offers any aid in accepting the unacceptable. I wandered in circles. My real life was underground, and even the dog park acreage stretched out before me like a graveyard.

ぐ

The first semester after Rajiv died I was assigned a section of Literary Criticism. Weeks four and five comprised a unit on psychoanalytic criticism. I wrote key terms on the board: the unconscious, repression, projection, transference. I taught students the theory that the mind protectively represses full knowledge of a trauma too painful to bear full-on, but that there was always, at least according to guru Freud, an inevitable "return of the repressed." Determined to break through the barrier to consciousness, repressed material gets smuggled across in disguised forms, appearing as dream images, jokes, or those infamous slips of the tongue, among other even more masked forms, which simultaneously reveal and conceal their true meaning. Beware the return of the repressed.

Unconscious mechanisms, I told the class, can work on a cultural level, too, according to some cultural critics. Myths act as cultural dreams, offering concealing revelations of repressed cultural anxieties or traumas that are too cruel to face head-on.

I myself was not a psychoanalytic critic, which required a faith beyond my rationalist ethic. So in spite of my teachings, I'd only understood repression as a sign of weakness. But now I found myself lauding it. "Repression is the most important of all psychoanalytic functions," I said unplanned. "It's what enables us to bear the unbearable."

My students' faces were blank, unimpressed with my rhapsody on repression. "A primary repression is our knowledge of death," I informed them. But, like me at twenty years old, they couldn't believe that they were ever going to die, and devoted themselves to their various myths of immortality. They're not unique; we all repress that awesome impasse, even we mourners. Can anyone really face such knowledge, or would the very sight of it strike us blind?

⟲

Six years later, back from visiting my mother-in-law in Kolkata, I was still unable to make any sense out of Rajiv's suffering and death. It was as if I had lost my place in the story of our lives and would never get back on track for the resolution. I lived in fragments seeking connection.

One summer day I wandered into the Humane Society under the pretext of donating rejected dog toys, which my three canines were now too old to play with. But something in my unconscious—the unconscious I didn't entirely believe in—was directing me toward new life.

The intake clerk told me that in her last home, Olive, the velvety black dog I tapped through cage bars, had been left alone all day, tied to a tree. That's no way to treat any dog, she said, much less a Border collie, the smartest and most hyperactive of all breeds. My rescue fantasies were prodded. This dog needed to learn how to love and to trust. I would give her a second life.

In the adoption room, Olive rolled on her back and exposed her white underbelly's bright blue hysterectomy tattoo. Her papers said that she had never given birth, but the clerk said it looked like she might have. Did she miss her babies? Did her belly remember their forms under her scar?

As soon as we got home, Olive attacked Blinky, my remaining cat, whose hissing made the Border collie all the more eager. Then she turned on Houdini. She held her head dominantly over Pretzel until he slunk back, shaking, and then, when Chappy tried to hold his head over her and protect the others, she pinned him down until he squealed. When I struggled to roll her over, she scratched and kicked, etching my arms and face. I clawed back.

Eventually she submitted. But only to me.

When I brought Olive to the dog park to try to work off some of her energy, she snapped at puppies who licked her face. She bit at the legs of dogs she herded and snarled at a submissive golden retriever. Over her dog's yelps, the owner yelled at me, "It says no aggressive dogs here. You are in violation." Other people turned to stare at me, now a criminal. Olive wagged her tail, looking for fresh evil.

Poor Pretzel hid behind heavy furniture overnight. When I coaxed him out in the morning, Olive lunged.

Nobody messes with my Pretzel. "You've snarled your last snarl at us," I told Olive in the car on the way back to the Humane Society. She licked her black muzzle.

The clerk, barely able to meet my eyes, handed me a form to sign, declaring that I was surrendering Olive to be euthanized if she was deemed unadoptable. Why would she be unadoptable now when she was adoptable the day before? Because I'd said that she snarled at other dogs. "I'll be honest," she added. "The odds aren't good for Olive."

So I kept her. Poor Pretzel.

The ensuing days revealed no dormancy to her wolf genes and the prey drive they expressed. On our daily trips to the dog park, she shook with excitement at the gate, and when it opened she was a sprung arrow, running with an urgency so desperate in its excitement that she emitted squeak-toy shrieks—or were they war cries? She ran back and forth at the fence and herded everything that moved. Her intensity bordered on bloodthirst. The dog park was her battlefield, and she was everywhere at once, a holy terror.

"Could you make your dog stop barking, *please*? It's hurting my ears." This was hissed to me more than once at the dog park, where, once the admired owner of cuddly spaniels, I was now shunned. I kept hoping Olive would bark herself into laryngitis, but instead her throat muscles only seemed to strengthen and gather force.

Olive backwards is Evil-O. And soon, to me, she became "The Evil One," along with the epithets "She-devil" and "Satan's Spawn." I knew intellectually, of course, that she wasn't evil; she was a force of nature, beyond good and evil—or perhaps *before* them. Indeed, her amorality inspired awe. But it's very hard for a human to comprehend pure action without intention.

I learned how to pull her out from under dog-piles, the taste of fight still hot in her mouth, the air charged with snarls. I learned to ignore the growls around me and stare her down until her upper lips dropped back down over her fangs. Our stand-offs regularized into ritual.

One day, spooked, she'd snarled at a husky, who'd come at her from behind. He instantly pinned her down. She fought more fiercely, her growls vibrating through her ribcage. I reached her just before blood flowed, and pulled her out with one hand while holding the husky with the other.

I glowered at Olive. Her tongue burned red against her black fur. She panted. I panted. She lowered her head and stared me down. But this time, as we huffed in oppositional rhythms, her form dilated into another, crueler figure, now laboring to metamorphose. Something bigger than a Border collie with a tongue hanging out, something beyond this moment, ancient and unfinished.

Kali. There she stood, the repressed returning with a red vengeance, batik made flesh. The heat of her tongue against black fur panting.

Who was this Kali, and why was she haunting me in the form of a Border collie? When I got home from the dog park that day, I searched through my India trunk for my stash of Amar Chitra Katha comics. I'd bought them from a bookseller's stall in Kolkata to try to learn Hindu mythology, but with every god an avatar of another god who had other avatars, I'd given up understanding years ago and packed the comics away. Now I dug them out again. I had no comics on Kali in particular, but I did remember something about her being an avatar of Durga, consort of Shiva, the Destroyer.

On the cover of Tales of Durga, a stunningly beautiful, many-armed Wonder Woman, clad in a bikini-like sari blouse and hourglass figure, sat smiling atop a lion. One arm thrusted a spear into a man-headed buffalo, while the other nine held various instruments of pain. Inside, the comic book depicted *asuras*, or demons, who threatened to take over the world. So Shiva, Vishnu, and Brahma, the Hindu trinity, concentrated their energies into a single beam to produce a goddess capable of defeating the *asuras*. The cover showed her in triumph after fierce, voluptuous battle.

But always the *asuras* returned. In the next battle, they were too much even for Durga as they endlessly multiplied: every time a drop of the blood of the great demon Raktabija touched the ground, another demon sprang up.

Like a cancer cell gone metastatic, I thought.

So Kali was produced, sprouting in parthenogenesis out of Durga's brow (or, more precisely, her "frown") in the midst of battle, born hungry for the kill. Kali spread her enormous, all-encompassing tongue across the battlefield and drank each drop of the demons' blood before it landed. Then, drunk with blood, she embarked on a demon-killing spree and adorned herself with a necklace of skulls and a skirt of severed arms.

That's as far as the comic book version went. I suspected there was more.

I now started reading in earnest. During the two hours a day I was spending in the dog park trying to tire Olive out—though all her running only seemed to engender new energy—I read alternately about Border collies and Hindu deities. Like Durga, all the female avatars of Shiva's goddess consort are more than a little wild, more than a little cruel. They are amoral, beyond good and evil, which—to a Westerner mired in Manichean dualism—looks a lot like evil. But all the other consorts of Shiva and their avatars are beautiful—almost pornographically so in the comics—except Kali, who is ugly, hideous even. Like Shiva, she has a third eye in the middle of her forehead. Always, her tongue is hanging out, lolling and red against her dark skin.

I read, too, about Bengalis' special connection to Kali, whom they worship as Kali-ma, the great Goddess Mother. In Bengali images especially, she is depicted as deeply black, against which her three red eyes are set off more dramatically. The name of Kolkata itself may be a corruption of Kalighat, one of her temples. One legend has it that when Kali's body was once cut up into pieces and scattered over the earth, her vagina landed in Bengal. I wondered where her tongue landed.

All of these accounts of Kali that I was reading insisted that she was *not* the goddess of death. (There was a god of death, Yama, but he was something else entirely.) Or if Kali did have some dominion over death, they said, it was the more metaphorical death of illusion. I tried to understand this distinction as I looked at images of Kali adorned with skulls and limbs, thirsty for more. Kali was instead, they said, a goddess of creation and destruction—a destruction that was somehow positive, as enabling as it was terrifying. "Her dark color is the color of the earth that creates life through constant destruction." But how could destruction be admired?

I tried to find the creative element, but she remained for me a goddess of death, black and red. Still, hunched on the dog park bench, I stared at her images. The intensity. The darkness. The tongue. She stared back at me with the third eye in her forehead.

"Don't look into her eye," I warn friends when they first meet Olive. Border collies are known for their intense stare. When a Border collie lowers its head to focus on its stalkee, it "has eye." That's what the shepherds call it: "eye" in the singular, as if the stare radiates from the middle of their forehead in a single, concentrated beam. The "eye" freezes sheep and hypnotizes cattle. Once you've looked into the eye, you will never be the same.

Riding into battle, Kali shrieks. Her call for battle, I read, is the pure and intense concentration of sound-energy into one awesome, earth-rocking "Om."

Charging over the dog park, Olive outran her own shrieks, running with the urgency of a joy indistinguishable from despair. Her wildness was so this-worldly that it was otherworldly.

At home, alone and uncrated while I was at work, Olive disinterred my photo boxes and gored through old pictures of Rajiv for which I had no negatives. When she ran out of these, she committed ritual sacrifice on my books, breaking their spines and leaving her dental imprints in their dismembered remains.

Kali once ate an elephant in battle. She ate swords and spears. She gained her strength from drinking the blood of *asuras*. She ate whole armies, then laughed in anger.

Taming the beast became my new life's purpose. Obedience classes taught positive reinforcement through treats and clicker training. *Sit-stay, down-stay, wait*. Olive proved to be wicked-smart, and picked up each new command with zeal, and then snatched the offered reward with equal ferocity. My thumb and index fingernails started cracking against Olive's enclosing teeth.

"Don't bite the hand that feeds you," the teacher said to Olive on the evening we began *heel*. I looked down to see a line of blood down my thumb, and below it, waiting expectantly, was the She-devil, staring, insistently, not at my thumb at all but at the treat beneath it. Her jaws parted.

Heel was the sticking point. Olive would not submit. My thumbs scabbed over.

Then one day in class Olive and I seemed to "get" heel at the same moment, to feel what it meant to move as a team, dog and left leg as one. I understood the exact moment to reward her, while she was still with me, connected and alert, and understood the exact moment to release her before she got bored.

The moment I gave Olive the release command, she attacked a Chihuahua.

Slowly, over months of obedience work, Olive and I bonded. Some of her traumatic past left her, but the Border collie remained. She was pure dog, in a way that my aging spaniels would never be. In the dog park she began to come in bounds when called, her back straight as an arrow shot from Shiva's famous bow, her nose targeting the bull's-eye treat in my hand. We showed off a little, even just to ourselves when no one else was in the park, attempting "comes" around obstacles and clear across the acreage. People stared at the black streak flaming over the snow. "Good girl," I'd say casually, thrilling inside.

But one winter day she didn't come when I called. Instead, she disappeared behind the cement tunnel. I put down my Kali reading. She was digging her nose into the deep snow and shaking her head, almost comically, in an exaggerated, cartoon-style "no." The object of fixation: a tiny mouse, struggling at paw's length away from Olive. Olive enjoyed the spectacle for moment, then picked up the mouse with her front teeth, gave it another good shake, and tossed it a few feet away. Like a cat, she toyed with its dying, killing it in increments for pure pleasure.

I swallowed a scream, one that threatened to be girly and high-pitched and suited to a cocker owner, but not a Border collie owner. By now I knew from my reading that Olive was merely exhibiting the Border collie motor patterns of hypertrophied chase drive with muted grab-bite-kill drive. But my motor patterns registered the action as torture.

I decided I should kill the mouse completely. But my attempts to get it away from Olive seemed to offend her ethics. It was her catch. She carried the mouse towards the other dogs, tossed and recaught it in front of them, then paraded around with her catch's wormy tail squirming out the side of her black lips.

Not till it was finally dead did she deign to let me investigate. I scooped the stiff body into a black poop-bag-turned-body-bag and threw it away. Olive looked at me with hurt and betrayal and puzzlement. Like I was a foreign and bizarre species incapable of rational behavior or higher understanding. Or like I'd wasted a kill.

I stared back. Just as I've started to love her again, I thought, to feel tender, even to believe it reciprocal, she remembers the call of Kali and the delirium of blood.

But I knew that wasn't the whole truth. I knew it when the brawny owner of a brawny lab said, "Wow, did she just catch a mouse? I'm impressed." As his dog seemed to be too, stepping aside as Olive ran by. If I were truthful, I would admit to the warm glow I'd felt at Olive's prowess, in spite of the single-digit temperature, in spite of my squeamishness at dead bodies and horror at the injustice of needless death, in spite of my humanity.

Some accounts say that Kali's tongue represents her omnivorousness. But others offer an alternate story: When Kali's killing spree got out of hand, Lord Shiva tried to stop her by throwing himself under her feet. Kali was so surprised at this sight that she stuck her tongue out in astonishment, and it remains eternally extended over her naked and bloodied breasts.

This tongue bespeaks the true meaning of cruelty, which I was slowly beginning to comprehend, and to distinguish from evil. Kali is cruel in the way that Nature is cruel. Indifferent to human-defined justice, she can produce pain as easily as pleasure, and can destroy as easily as create.

In this sense of cruelty, Kali is the cruelest of all deities—and the most natural. She is not malicious or evil, nor is she benevolent. She just is.

In Bengal, Kali is the Dark Mother, with absolute love for her children, whom she is fierce to protect.

Border collies were selectively bred to retain all the predatory instinct of their wolf ancestors, but to turn it toward fiercely protective ends.

One recent spring day in the dog park with Olive and Houdini, when I'd had the Evil One for almost a year—by now she'd long accepted my other dogs as her family—a pit bull, who'd been good-natured and goofy, flipped into bloodlust, and his mouth closed over Houdini's neck. Houdini squealed more unearthly shrieks than Olive ever did, but these were the shrieks of pure terror, not of power.

Olive sprung to action, the terrible and avenging childless mother. She stuck her nose into the pit bull's face and let loose her high-pitched, unearthly shriek. In an instant, the pit pinned her down and barked into her neck, spewing spittle across her forehead. Like Kali atop Shiva, I thought, in that first split second; but something wasn't right. Olive should be the one on top.

Olive kept shrieking, unwilling to submit even as she was pinned to the ground, even as the pit's jaw moved in to her throat. I tugged the pit off, growling and hackled and foaming. I didn't think or hesitate, just reached in and tugged. After the adrenaline subsided, I realized how fierce a move that was, but at the time it just felt factual.

Just as I pulled the startled dog off, Olive sprang back up snarling, and as I moved in to block her from the pit bull, she hit me in the nose with her bared teeth. Blood spurted. My blood, I realized, and oddly felt like laughing. It was my first true bloody nose, and

I was amazed at the abundance of red that poured out. Grabbing Olive's collar, I sneezed red droplets onto her black fur.

As the pit bull owner dragged his dog off, Olive rose from the ground, bejeweled in bloodstones. Houdini, finally understanding that he was saved, stopped yelping and took refuge between my legs. Olive and I stared each other down. Both our chests were heaving. With her third eye trained on my limited two, something moved in me, inside of the pain and panting. It alerted my muscles and bones and neurons with an urgency I could barely remember. It was a feeling from long ago. It was life.

We're most alive when we're standing right on top of death, balancing with bare feet on its bare body.

To live with the presence of death. To recognize and respect nature's cruelty. To know that the real cruelty, the necessary cruelty, is that life goes on. That I, too, will live on, even under death's gaze and encircled by skulls, because life is as relentless as death, as indifferent and unremitting—which may be the most gruesome truth of all.

As I finish writing this piece, I do what I had not yet been able to: I unearth the batik Kali from the India trunk. The image is bigger than I remembered, too wide to hang on the door as I'd planned, so I spread it out on my bed. There she lies, in her beautiful, ten-handed, Mahakali version, floating in a sea of red matching her bloodied chest. I may never understand Kali in the true Hindu sense. But I understand in my own way her garland of skulls, her skirt of severed arms, and her red tongue lolling, thirsty for blood, as she roams the cremation grounds. I dare to wonder if this is how Rajiv connected with her in those last few days of meditation before her image, the concentrated knowledge so heavy between his eyes that it bowed his head. In spite of my Jewish-atheist beliefs, I realize, I'd still harbored longings for redemption. Ensconced in a Christian culture, I can't help but expect a pay-off at the end, to feel that a narrative should end in the closure of salvation. I've been too Western to accept the fact of death without compensation. But I am beginning to replace Christ with Kali. I am remembering how the light flooded in through the living room window to reach Rajiv's head, bowed before the goddess, and how it burned his black hair red.

"Once you understand Kali," instructs one follower of the goddess, "you are no longer afraid of her awesome powers of creation and destruction. You accept." But no, I do not accept, not yet, maybe not ever. For now, I respect.

As I pin the batik Kali back up on our wall, where it once hung, the three older dogs sniff at it with mobile noses. Do they recognize the scent from seven years ago, when I, or someone who I used to be, took the tapestry down with trembling hands? Or has the smell transmuted?

Olive doesn't sniff; she stands alert, then lowers her head into stalking pose to give it the eye. Kali matches her gaze with Border collie intensity. They are frozen in a stare-down, third eye to third eye.

5

Old Dogs' Tricks

In the August heat, twelve-year-old Pretzel hounds an uncut pit bull across the four-acre dog park. When the pit pauses for a breather, Pretzel seizes his chance, mounts the pit's flanks, and humps. A little girl squeals. Other bystanders howl with laughter at the gyrating hips of my arthritic, leggy, black spaniel mix. The pit bull seems barely to notice, though his jaw drops into a grin. "Pretzel!" I scold. "Stop that!" But I'm faking it. I'm always a little glad for him when he successfully mounts; it gives him such dog-joy.

"Turbo! Goddam you!" a man growls. "Don't you dare be anyone's bitch." He turns to me. His red beard is punctuated by a black plug in each ear lobe, and his scalp is swathed in a black bandana with delicate white spots which, when I squint, reveal themselves as shrunken skulls. Like Pretzel, I have a soft spot for pit bulls, who regularly defy their belligerent reputation, so I'm always a little disappointed when the pit bull owners persist in upholding theirs. "Will you get your dog off my dog?" He stares me down. I suspect that if I were male, or twenty years younger even, his address to me might have been more colorful.

"I'm trying," I offer, demonstrating incompetence as I reach for

Pretzel's collar, while Turbo, twice my dog's thirty pounds, shrugs Pretzel off and scampers away, unconcerned about his sexual identity.

Pretzel's cloudy eyes, bulging under the crescents of his now-white eyebrows, look confused. At twelve, he's losing his sight and his hearing, though not, apparently, his libido, even though he's been neutered for eleven years. Missing the pit bull, he sidles up to Turbo's thirty-something goth-biker-pirate owner to lure a petting out of him, but the man in the black bandana only glares back at Pretzel's hungry spaniel eyes.

Pretzel needs love. He may be old, but he's eternally floppy-eared, clambering to connect more than to dominate. So he scans the dog park for other possibilities, spots the pig-tailed little girl, and edges up to her. But she shrieks into his face, "Eeww, this one's old." Pretzel, my dog of Dr. Seussian disproportions, shows the snaggle-tooth jutting out of his underbite. When he was young, his flaws were cute. But no more, apparently. "It's old, it's old," the girl shrieks again, and pulls away. Pretzel's tail dips, with just a tad of hopeful wag still animating the white tip.

Turbo rumbles past again, so fast that Pretzel can only take an ineffectual lunge at him before wandering on to another man he's caught sight of. I've been watching this man for a while. He's about my age—late forties—or possibly a tad younger, but just a tad, with his still mostly brown hair sprouting gray at the temples. But the woman he's been flirting with is half our age. Unlike me in my full-length jeans wilting in the heat, she's wearing cut-offs and her legs are flawless. A future of cellulite or varicose veins is unthinkable to her, I suspect; she can't imagine herself ever being anything but young. She's a Brittany. Not the dog breed, but the human one; I call females of her demographic "the Brittanys," because that's what they're all named, if they're not Ashleys or Lindsays—just as my generation of women are Debbies and Lisas and Jills. She's concentrating on the man's stories about Hewlett-Packard, where, he lets it be known, he's a systems engineer, and she laughs encouragingly, oblivious to the overheated chocolate lab plopped at her feet in the sliver of shade made by her shadow. A beagle—"Murphy"—intermittently runs up to the HP man to check in, then resumes his phantom chase. As a middle-aged woman, I am even more invisible to both of these humans than their dogs are.

Pretzel positions himself in front of Murphy's dad and waits. Moves closer. Moves closer yet. But Murphy's dad is oblivious to all the dogs, and certainly to old Pretzel. He's fixated on Brittany. Pretzel is now leaning against Murphy's dad's legs, but the man won't bend.

Pretzel breaks his stance only when Turbo sweeps back into view. Pretzel can't help it; he lunges, misses, recovers, and trots off after Turbo. I look for Turbo's dad, and see that he's been watching all three of us, so I pretend to run after the dogs to monitor. "Sorry," I mumble to the man in the black bandana as I jog by with exaggerated middle-aged ineffectuality. "Pretzel likes un-neutered males."

"My dog's not gay," snaps bandana man.

"But mine is," I sigh.

It's true. Pretzel can't keep his paws off an uncut male. He's always liked males better than females, human or canine. Way back when he was a puppy, and I a young woman, and we lived as a family with our man Rajiv, the love of my life, and also the love of Pretzel's, I was annoyed at my pup's misdirected allegiance; I was the one who had initially wanted a dog—no, needed one, with maternal rabidity—the one who walked him and cleaned up his poop and took him to the vet. But from the moment Rajiv leaned over the skinny black dog's cage at the Humane Society and said, "How about this one?" (to which I'd answered, "Too big."), Pretzel was fixed on his master, and I learned to accept second-place status, which was not too bad, since both Pretzel and Rajiv had a lot of love to spare. For six years, Pretzel stayed a puppy.

Then came cancer. Within months, Pretzel lost his puppyhood while Rajiv aged in dog years. Starting at thirty-seven, Raju became an old man in ten months, and then a dying man, his cinnamon skin stained yellow with bilirubin as his liver tumors bred. Pretzel lost his bounce and settled into Rajiv's rhythms. Photos from Rajiv's last year always show Pretzel at his side, curled into the deepening hollow of his stomach. To the very end. Rajiv died at home, with me by his side, and Pretzel curled at the foot of the hospice-supplied bed I'd set up downstairs. He lay in vigil at his master's feet until the last breath.

After his master's death, Pretzel crawled under the couch and his face turned white—almost that quickly. For days he refused to eat—or if he did he threw up. For weeks Pretzel lay low, crouching, holding himself uncharacteristically aloof from the strangers who streamed through the house, and taking little interest in the outside noises that he used to monitor from the window. After years of being perfectly housetrained, he became temporarily incontinent and began to pee in the same spot in the living room over and over. Then one day I realized what that spot meant: it was where the hospice bed had been set up, the spot where Rajiv died. Pretzel was marking his loss.

I, too, aged in dog years as I mourned. Rajiv died five days after I turned thirty-nine. Overnight I doubled in age, joining the ranks of geriatric widows with whom I now identified. We were a sect whose members dwelled in truths our culture anxiously denies:

that death is everywhere; that a lifetime goes by so quickly it's as if we all age in dog years.

Sometimes the loneliness was animal, a body hunger, an epithelial craving for touch. If you don't feel yourself touched by another, how do you know your contours, your outline? How do you keep from evaporating into air? Nobody had told me about the need so muscular that the word "desire" would never do.

Pretzel must have felt this loss of touch too, a fur-hunger to match my skin-hunger, no matter how much I petted and stroked him. When we started going back to the dog park, he sought out men more doggedly than ever. He'd seek affection from everyone, but especially from men, whom he'd stand in front of and eye meaningfully, maybe even show a little tongue, until he got a head-pat or maybe even a butt-rub, making his tail wag in double-time.

One theory about tail-wagging is that it serves to spread anal scents, enveloping others into the dog's reality, sharing molecules of information and intimacy. Dogs breathe each other in. So much more engrossing than a handshake and exchange of names, it's an act of fundamental generosity and openness, an invitation to smell and to know. What a dog wants most is to mingle his scents with another, to smell and be smelled.

Does Pretzel remember Rajiv at all? If Rajiv walked in the door right now, Pretzel would be ecstatic, jumping outside his skin, like in the old days when Rajiv came back after a conference or field trip and Pretzel leapt over himself in circles. But as he ages, Pretzel moves through grief, too, in dog years, and he's now on the other side.

At his recent check-up, Dr. Foster said Pretzel seemed to be doing well "for his age." When she asked about arthritis, I said, "No sign of it," with perhaps a touch of pride. But when she manipulated his back legs he jumped and started. "Early arthritis," she pronounced. I bought a sixty-dollar tub of glucosamine treats, which, she said, "should make him feel a whole lot better. You'll notice a difference in just a few days."

How did I miss it? In the days that followed, I noticed that Pretzel doesn't much like his butt petted anymore, and he doesn't jump on and off the furniture as much. He hasn't been scampering up and down the stairs every time I do, but waits to see if I'm going to stay. He's been in pain, and I've been blind to it. I've only seen his whitening face. Pretzel is officially old, and aging more every day. In his rear years. For a while after that veterinary visit, every time I caught his eye I apologized to him.

Now at the dog park Pretzel moves deeper into the crowd of humans, looking for love. He pursues the twenty-something woman shielding the girl and brushes his tail across her knees. He waits. He searches her face earnestly to see what's causing the delay. She notices him, bends her head, and says with over-enunciation, "You're old." Pretzel looks to her even more earnestly and wags even more energetically. She tries again. "You're an old dog," she pronounces, then looks away. Pretzel keeps wagging his tail even as it droops.

The heat is almost unbearable as Pretzel settles back at my side, the spine under his hot black fur softening at my touch. I'm back to watching the human mating ritual with fascination, disgust, and envy, when Pretzel's tail instantly stiffens, and I simultaneously jump at the scruff-raising male voice behind me.

"Get your dog the fuck off my dog." It's bandana man. He's found someone more opportune than a middle-aged woman to pick a fight with: Murphy's dad, the HP man, who's nearly engineered a date with Brittany. It seems that Murphy the beagle, too, has taken a liking to the uncut Turbo and is going at it with youthful alacrity while Turbo, unperturbed, catches his breath through a dog smile.

"Fuck you," the engineer shouts back. Brittany's giggles sound like hiccups.

"Fuck *you*," returns bandana man, "And fuck your dog." You can practically smell his testosterone.

"What an asshole," Brittany mumbles to HP man, loud enough for bandana man to hear. "He should leave."

"Get the hell out," Mr. HP shouts on Brittany's behalf. "This place is for dogs, not assholes."

"Then leave, bitch."

"You leave."

The hairs on the backs of their necks hackle. Turbo, meanwhile, has turned and is humping Murphy back with full-wagging tail.

Bandana man breaks the stare-down. "I'll wait for you outside. I'ma kick your ass."

"Fuck you." Murphy's owner pulls his beagle out from under the pit bull.

Bandana man harnesses Turbo and shouts from the gate, "You come settle this outside. If you have the balls."

By now Pretzel is opportunely humping Murphy. I take an exaggerated feint at pulling him off. Now, unless he wants to fight the pirate, Murphy's owner will have to notice me, or at least notice Pretzel. "I guess you're going to have to beat *me* up now," I offer to Murphy Senior. My diversion is a gift, and he should know it. I stare at him with Border collie expectation. We're all squinting in the sun. Next to young Brittainy, I feel the crow's feet form around my eyes, and then see the same formations around his, like crosshatched, hieroglyphic characters. His eyes, which were brown, now offer green and gold. For a moment, they meet mine.

Then they roll past me to the dog pile, and he shrugs. "They're dogs." He knees Pretzel off Murphy, which leaves my dog tottering, so he grabs Pretzel's harness to steady him, and speaks directly into Pretzel's cloudy eyes, "You know, old-timer, you really are too old to be chasing after these young guys." He turns to Brittany, who smiles approvingly. He's won her back. Bandana man is forgotten.

Pretzel looks uncertain, but, thrilled for any male attention at all, he unfurls his tail and waves it full-masted, spreading out his anal scents in an invitation to all who would partake. Amidst stronger, more pungent, more dog-sweet smells, the invitation lingers in the heat.

6

Scavenger Love

Every time the Animal Control van crept down my block, I'd mutter an atheist's prayer that it wouldn't stop at my house. As a childless widow with four dogs, I'd become the neighborhood Crazy Dog Lady. It was only a matter of time before I reached the extremity documented on reality television shows.

I don't know if or when my relationship with dogs became unnatural, or unhealthy, or maybe just weird. Animal behavioral scientist Temple Grandin says that "animals make us human," but my dogs made me a little less human. When you live with dogs long enough, you forget that they're another species, and that their ways—sniffing crotches, mauling underwear, licking snot, scavenging garbage—should be seen as uncouth, even disgusting. At night, dogs settled into the empty space in the bed still sagging to my late husband's shape even after all these years, and I fell asleep to the clicking of teeth on buffalo bones. On bad days, when grief surged and I buried my head in my pillow to muffle my sobs, I had to pause occasionally to pick dog hairs out of my mouth.

By the tenth anniversary of Rajiv's death, black and tan dog hairs became so deeply embedded in my now-gray carpets that their original ocean blue color was irrecoverable.

How do you know when you've crossed the line of acceptable human-dog relations? At what point does the van stop for you?

Determining the proper relationship between humans and dogs has a renewed urgency in our current cultural moment of unprecedented pet ownership, but it has probably troubled humans since the origin of dogs as a (sub)species. We often look to nature and "the natural" for guidance in such matters, but the natural history of dogs is still under disputed construction.

Probably around ten to fifteen thousand years ago, but possibly (according to some mitochondrial DNA evidence) up to thirty thousand, dogs emerged as the first domesticated nonhuman animal. Some anthrozoologists conjecture that the entire species is human-made from the start; others believe that dogs evolved on their own, filling a niche through natural selection, long before humans began selectively breeding. It's even possible that dogs evolved twice, or even three separate times in different parts of the world. They may have evolved from proto-wolves, maybe in northern Asia or maybe the Middle East or perhaps even Europe. All we know for certain—or think we do—is that dogs evolved alongside humans, intertwined with human interests from their beginnings, leading to this bizarre hybrid of natural selection and human engineering.

I'm most charmed by the hypothesis that, as humans, we've evolved to melt over creatures with large eyes and heads bigger than their bodies. When early humans came upon lairs of abandoned wolf-pups, the story goes, the most nurturing of the humans—probably women—kept the pups as pets. The most submissive, trusting, and pedomorphic (maintaining childlike features into adulthood) of the wolves were allowed to stay among the humans and to eat their food scraps. In only ten or so generations, wolf ears began to flop and bellies to whiten. If dogs as a (sub)species are man-made, were they ever "natural"?

On the other hand, an increasingly accepted theory, and the one I find most compelling, is the scavenger theory, which postulates that dogs evolved from wolves as super-scavengers. Some wolves may have begun to forage around the outskirts of early villages and to feed on humans' scraps. Over time, the least reactive to human activity would have fared better and would have repopulated around the dump sites. Humans benefited from this clean-up service, and would have tolerated the increasingly mellow wolves who posed little threat, and even provided rudimentary protection. Gradually, humans and dogs began to live in cautious, symbiotic proximity.

Consistent with their scavenger origins, dogs' mouths are the hearts of their being, while their bodies are consummate eating machines. This oral fixation enables us to train them, seduce them, bond with them. Our species communicate with each other through food and tongues. It's a relationship of the mouth and the belly. Dogs' mouths also serve as hands, grasping; their tongues are both palms and fingers. They communicate more with mouth and tongue than with vocal cords, expressive as their barks may be. A licking is both touch and speech: an oral sign language of licks, an interspecies *lingua franca*.

While zoologists explain face-licking as the legacy of the pups' attempts to stimulate their mamas to vomit pre-digested meals into their mouths, I relished the touch of a tongue, the intimacy of a lick, the language of scavenger love.

It was a lick that made Rajiv's mortality real. Soon after he turned thirty-seven years old, and Pretzel, our black spaniel mix, turned five, Rajiv went to the doctor about his sudden hemorrhoids and was diagnosed with Stage IV colon cancer accompanied by metastatic tumors in all four quadrants of his liver. Checked into the hospital. Tests and biopsies. Terminal. He would get a port installed, start chemo and radiation, and maybe extend his life by a year.

We were in shock. When I took breaks from the hospital to let out and feed our two dogs, Pretzel kept looking past me for Rajiv. In the hospital for days, Rajiv stayed in his white nightmare without respite.

Finally, he was discharged. The whole car ride home, Rajiv kept his eyes closed. He still seemed dazed when I pulled into the garage. But when I opened the door and Pretzel came running out, Rajiv woke up.

Pretzel's whole back—not just his tail—was wagging, making half-circle arcs. He jumped into Rajiv's lap as soon as he opened the car door. Rajiv staggered out of the car and onto the garage door steps. Pretzel jumped back and forth over Rajiv and pushed his head under Rajiv's armpit so he could lick Rajiv's left ear.

That's when Rajiv lost it. Crying into Pretzel's black fur as his tail wound around like a propeller.

Because dogs scavenged corpses along with other refuse, they have been associated with death in many cultural traditions, or sometimes serve as intermediaries between life and death (or afterlife). In the Hindu tradition of Rajiv's upbringing, two four-eyed dogs help Yama, the God of Death, guard the gates of the otherworld. In Greek mythology, Cerberus, a three-headed dog, stood guard at the gates of Hades, where he let souls in but not out. The ancient Egyptians worshipped Anubis, the jackal-god and guide into the Afterlife, and the Aztecs had Xolotl, a sometimes monstrous dog of the Underworld. Throughout the British Isles, even to this day, various legends of "The Black Dog" have proliferated. This real or phantom dog appears, often with red eyes, to portend a coming death or to escort a new soul to the underworld.

If it's true that myths are a culture's dreams, and that, like dreams, they both reveal and conceal repressed truths, then these mythic dogs point to a recognition that human-dog relations exceed the natural realm, and venture into the supernatural, the nebulous realm of instinct and intuition that some people call the spiritual world. In the human imagination, dogs sit at that liminal space between human civilization, such as it is, and the natural world to which we all return. Dogs show us the way to a world beyond our knowing.

All through Rajiv's illness and treatment, Pretzel lay by his side, his head nuzzled under Rajiv's armpit.

When Rajiv went into liver failure, we set up a hospice bed in the living room. Pretzel curled up in a ball, pretzel-style, at Rajiv's feet and kept vigil. After his master died, Pretzel crouched under the futon for nearly two weeks (far past the seven days of sitting *shiva* from my Jewish heritage, and longer even than the ten days for *sraddh* from Rajiv's Hindu heritage). The little black dog barely ate, and when he did, he vomited. My own body hungered without appetite.

For months after Rajiv's death I felt a bit like a black dog myself. Inhabiting the edges of the living world, among humans but not quite of them, I had a foot in the world of the dead. As a raw widow, I also connoted death to other humans, who I sometimes caught turning their heads away and pretending not to have seen me, so that they wouldn't get stuck in a conversation conspicuously avoiding the subject of death. I was just as happy not to talk to them and preferred the company of my dogs, who never left me shaking in the wake of metaphysical consolations like "God has a plan" or "Everything happens for a reason" or "He's in a better place," platitudes that may comfort believers but can only increase a nonbeliever's isolation. Instead, my growing dog pack merely sniffed my pant legs for leftover crumbs, or poked probing noses into my pockets, licking my hungry skin with spongy tongues, offering me the comforts of scavengers, forcing me out of *if only* and into *now*.

By then, Pretzel had long resumed eating. How could he not? But I still can't explain his period of fasting as anything other than mourning. If Pretzel, the consummate scavenger, refused food, then something beyond food-seeking marks dogs' relationships to us.

At those generative dump sites thousands of years ago, the dogs who could best adjust to the whims of humans would have disproportionately passed along their human-sensitive genetic lines. Dogs' sympathy for humans runs deep in their DNA. They search our faces for signs and read our gestures. They know what we're thinking even when we're unaware that we've physicalized our thoughts. When I merely consider going out, my Border collie runs to the door.

Humans learned how to exploit this sensitivity along with the more basic scavenger instinct. Once we began to generate new uses for dogs, selective breeding quickly overtook the glacial job of natural selection. But if selective breeding is not natural, are the resulting dogs natural? Is a cocker spaniel—or even a Border collie—natural? Can we call the roles for which we bred dogs natural? Are any dog-human relations beyond the scavenger-based one natural?

Most likely, the first role of working dogs was guarding flocks. People realized that dog pups raised among sheep would not see the latter as prey, but would bond with them and protect them from other predators. In other words, we bred dogs, at the start, to identify with other species, a confusion rarely seen "in nature." Dogs then enabled the pastoral lifestyle that became a hallmark of human civilizations. (Is human civilization "natural"?) Unnatural selection next bred for herders, retrievers, and trackers, as humans figured out how to refocus dogs' prey drive into designer niches, and how to refine dependence into faithfulness. We trained dogs to "unnaturally" (against their nature) identify with humans, so much so that they will relinquish their food to us.

Common lore concerning human relationships with dogs now puts pet-keeping as among the most recently evolved (and dubious) of canine roles. This belief often bolsters the charge that pet-keeping is "unnatural." But some newer evidence—including dogs buried in graves with humans, and the remains of dogs found within households—suggests that cohabitation and intimacy between humans and dogs might go back almost to their origins. This relationship between humans and household dogs, though, seems always to have been anxiety-ridden, especially when it threatened the primacy of the human-to-human relationship, and the dog became a family member.

After Rajiv died, I became that crazy dog lady, verging on hoarder. People thought me unnatural. Rajiv and I never wanted children, but a few years into our life together I'd gotten intense yearnings for a dog. They went beyond emotional; my whole body ached for canine companionship. I've heard other women describe baby longings, which I've never felt, but they sound a whole lot like my dog yearnings. To this day, I melt over puppies the way "normal" women melt over babies. If a puppy is in my vicinity I can't concentrate on anything else. Every spring brings stabbing dog urges, which only sharpened after Rajiv died, resulting in my four-dog household. I still have occasional PMS dreams of giving birth to a litter of puppies.

Familiarity breeds suspicion. One episode in the history of interspecies familiarity dramatizes such suspicion with particular clarity. In early modern Europe ("the Renaissance"), one of the signs of being a witch was the possession of a familiar (from the Latin *famulus*, a household servant or attendant). Also called a familiar spirit or animal familiar, this supernatural spirit taking physical form most often appeared as an animal, but sometimes as a humanoid creature, imp, faerie, or demon. The most common familiar animals were cats (such as the notorious black cat), dogs, owls, and toads, but witch trial histories also record mice, bats, ravens, lizards, and other animals. These familiars, often bearing affectionate nicknames, guarded, protected, and guided their human counterparts.

Roughly eighty percent of accused witches were women, generally middle-aged or otherwise non-procreative, who lived alone and almost certainly relied on the companionship of their indoor animals, as well as the protection that those animals gave through either brute force or early warnings from their access to sounds and smells beyond human perception. (This demographic bears striking resemblance to the typical profile of a modern-day hoarder or

Crazy Cat/Dog Lady.) Pets gave these women some independence. A non-procreative woman living alone would have been a very unnatural thing in early modern Europe. Perhaps having animals in the home, in close relationship with humans, appeared so unnatural as to seem freakish and in need of punishment. Perhaps feeding table scraps to household animals—giving them the same food eaten by humans—and letting dogs and cats sleep in bed, was going too far. Some witches were said to love their animal familiars over human babies, or even over their human family members. This unnatural blurring of species must have given clear proof of the devil at work.

Between ten and forty thousand people were executed as witches. Among these witches was the elderly, one-legged widow Elizabeth Clarke, who, subjected to "interrogation techniques" developed by witch-finder Matthew Hopkins, acknowledged the demon-nature of her familiars. Hopkins' 1647 book *The Discovery of Witches* recommends the infamous "water test," the cutting test, and many other techniques. It also notes another tell-tale sign of witch-hood: a witch often bore a "third teat," through which she nourished her familiars with milk or, in some accounts, with her own blood.

I can imagine a woman not that different from me living alone with her dogs, who, one day, prick up their ears, then launch into warning growls. Soon a wagon appears along the road bearing the witch-finder, his assistants, and their testing kit packed in a black bag. As the witch-finder opens the bag, the woman sees the gleam of a knife's blade. He tells her that if she confesses outright, he won't need to conduct his tests. She knows what they want to hear. But if she confesses, they will kill her dogs, who are even now circling around the strangers, waiting for her directive. She gives them the release command and motions for them to run away. Satisfied that they are beyond harm, she braces herself for the interrogation.

When Chappy, our blond cocker/Pomeranian/poodle mix, was a mischievous puppy, Rajiv called him "the imp." After Rajiv's death, Chappy, of all my dogs, behaved most like a self-appointed witch's imp. His personality changed overnight. Sensing my vulnerability, he stuck to my side, always facing outward and guarding me against unseen forces. When I was at rest, he lay not just beside me but on me, sometimes draped over my chest or burrowed under my legs. He saw to it that we always maintained contact, that I was always being touched. At a time when I doubted I was even alive and present in this physical world, he gave me shape.

Chappy continued for years to imp me with the same intensity, even as he became half- deaf, arthritic, and so tired that he often fell asleep standing up, his blond eyelashes clam-shelling his black pearl eyes as his eraser nose dropped into his chest.

I came to count on Chappy's presence in Raju's side of the bed, pressed up against my right side, holding me in place. Allowing dogs in bed troubles not just pet skeptics but also many dog trainers and behaviorists, who warn that it puts dogs on the same level as their human masters. Dogs need to be dogs, and people, people. The Monks of New Skete, for example, believe that you can't get control over your dogs if you entitle them as sleeping partners. Dogs-in-bed is the part of dog ownership that I generally admit only to other dog fanatics, and even then only in whispers. An interspecies family might not appear as sinful today as it did during witch trial times, but it's still socially policed as "unnatural."

Laid across my chest, Chappy's heartbeat summoned my own.

Sometimes he smelled like a sea bass, but most often he was a loaf of sourdough bread.

The modern-day equivalent of the witch-finder, at least for middle-aged women with hoarding tendencies, is the Animal Control agent, that object of my ongoing fears. I could imagine the Animal Control van stopping at my house. Perhaps the neighbors have complained about the barking, or the smell, or the sporadic poop removal. At least one of my dogs—Olive, whom I adopted after an accidental trip to the Humane Society—was taken from a hoarder. I imagined myself as that hoarder. I saw two men in uniform approaching my door. I let them in and played dumb. While my cocker, Houdini, boomeranged off their legs, while Pretzel butted his head under their hands to force a petting, while Chappy crooned his welcome howl, and while Olive barked and nipped at their shins, the men would ask me to voluntarily relinquish my dogs to the pound, where they would be evaluated for adoptability. The Animal Cops would ask me to submit to psychiatric evaluation. It would be for my own good.

I would not be as brave as my predecessors, Elizabeth Clarke and the others. I would snarl and rage and whimper and beg.

That feared visit from the Animal Control van never came. Instead, at thirteen years old, Chappy got cancer. When dogs stop eating, you know it's bad. I expended an inordinate amount of resources on surgery and medication—resources that, some friends noted, could have better gone to actual human beings. Three days after Chappy died, Pretzel, now over sixteen years old, collapsed. A previously symptomless tumor burst and bled internally. He would not recover.

Precious Memories Pet Cemetery and Crematory stretched out like Elysium Fields. The white tombstones arose from grass unbelievably green amidst our Colorado drought. Exotic flowers brocaded the perimeter. A pond, probably man-made, stretched west behind the tombstones. In the evening it would have reflected the sunset. For advocates of a firm line between humans and (other) animals, this pet cemetery would be golden evidence of devolution.

In spite of the campy opulence, I came undone.

To the woman inside the patio-turned-office, I said, "I'm here for my dogs." She exchanged my check for two flower-adorned urns, about a quarter the size of Rajiv's, which had been shockingly tiny. My dogs' urns were smaller than their chew toys.

I sent Pretzel's ashes down the same river in Rocky Mountain National Park that had swirled Rajiv's ashes ten years earlier. I've kept Chappy's remains. Chappy, my imp. I informed my closest friend, presumed executor of my unofficial will, that I want Chappy's ashes mixed with mine. That was a little too much interspecies mingling even for him; he couldn't bring himself to consent.

A couple of weeks after their deaths, I attended a Pet Memorial at the veterinary school where Pretzel died. I asked Kelley to come with me. A PowerPoint procession of our beloved pet photos backdropped poetry readings and professional condolences. A grief counselor assured us that it was normal to grieve acutely for one's pet, and that we shouldn't feel guilty if we find ourselves grieving more intensely for our animal companions than we have for, say, our own mothers. "Look around you," she said to the packed lecture hall. We comprised a menagerie, roughly eighty percent gray-and white-haired women, but also children, teenagers, and grown men, even rancher types with cowboy hats and leathery arms. All of us were bereft by the loss of our pets. All of us, the counselor said, were normal.

"This is weird," Kelley whispered to me. I yanked a tissue out of his hand.

Maybe all of us pet mourners are weird, or abnormal, or unhealthy, symptoms of a culture whose relationship to animals and nature has gone mutant. Maybe all of us in the lecture hall could have confessed to witchcraft.

Meanwhile Houdini, at eleven, was diagnosed with congestive heart failure and given six months to live.

I tried to train Olive to sleep by my side, in Rajiv's former spot, like Chappy used to, but Olive would have none of it, and insisted on demoting herself to the floor.

I began visiting Rescue and Adoption centers, "just to look," slipping my fingers between the metal bars and letting the abandoned dogs lick my fingers. I couldn't reach in any farther, but I connected with their tongues, some puppy-soft, some sandpaper rough, some delicate, some dripping. I preferred their sticky saliva to the isopropanol-based hand sanitizer with which I was supposed to decontaminate myself after our mouthy encounters. My first impulse had been to fill my house with rescue dogs, but I tried, strained, to wait for the one who silently called to me. One of them, soon, would make my third teat swell.

If I have crossed a line in my relations with dogs, I'm not going back. I can't imagine returning to a time before dogs. I can't imagine a life in which garbage was just garbage rather than an occasion for joy, or in which toilet paper rolls sat snug in their cubbies, or socks were safe, or pant legs innocent. I can't imagine extending an arm beneath the book I'm reading and not feeling a patch of warm fur settling under my hand. I would miss watching dogs' ears perk to ultrasonic music that I can't hear, or their noses bow to olfactory wonders I'll never know. I'd miss their calibrating noses, their probing, dexterous tongues, their insatiable appetites.

The connection between humans and dogs feels ancient, deep as DNA, primitive as scavenging, basic as hunger. Is it natural? Maybe the human-dog relationship exceeds and even bewilders a simple model of nature as something distinct from human culture. Perhaps our interspecies relationship is as natural and unnatural as the first civilization.

I sometimes imagine that first contact fifteen thousand years ago. The first human to physically connect with the increasingly domesticated scavenger wolves would, suggest some historians, most likely have been a woman. She would have been a bit of a scavenger herself. Perhaps a widow without children and past childbearing age. The community might have tolerated her, but she would have been the last served at meals. She often went hungry. Perhaps she only got her turn at the roast as the other humans left and the scavenging wolf-dogs moved in. The canines gradually accepted her presence, though there was little food to spare. Perhaps when times got better, she saved aside scraps for her favorites: for the older bitch, trying to hide her limp, who got pushed outside the feeding circle; or for the little pups deemed too weak to save. She may have preferred the most puppyish ones, those with the floppiest ears, highest yelps, and most sincere belly-exposing submissiveness.

Maybe the community, at first amused, grew suspicious. Rumors whispered that the widow was being improper with the dogs, that she was touching them on the head. Someone said they saw her pulling burrs out of the alpha male's thick coat. Someone else said that she had even been seen holding one of the pups in her arms like a newborn babe. When someone else swore to have seen the pups licking the widow's face, the elders decided she'd gone too far. This mixing with animals was unclean, unnatural, and offensive to the gods, not to mention just plain weird.

But on the day the men approached the widow among the dogs to forbid and sever these contacts, I imagine, the dogs smelled their hostility, and gathered around the widow, the most robust males in front, enlarging themselves with bristling scruffs. Even the old bitch stumbled forward to bare her yellowed teeth.

The men must have wondered at this loyalty, far stronger than any they'd seen among their kind. Perhaps they were a little awed. Perhaps they saw the hand of the gods intervening in their plans, telling them to accept these scavenger wolves as their own special species to re-make in their image. They obeyed. Perhaps, over time, the widow's bizarre attachment to these scavengers came to be seen as an eccentricity sanctioned by the gods.

Eventually it became natural.

7

Canine Cardiology

I'd always thought that Houdini, my cocker spaniel with a massive eating disorder, was doomed to a death by gorging. As a puppy, remember, he chomped books and tampons and tissues and paper clips and pencils, and later he devoured whole newspapers, their rubber bands and plastic bags still intact. Beyond bulimic, he gobbled back up his own vomit. He earned his name for his ability to get into anything, opening closed drawers and latched cabinet doors and, of course, garbage cans of every design. It turned out, though, that he couldn't get out of things as easily as he got into them.

Although my little garbivore could find food anywhere, it soon became obvious that he was as mentally challenged as he was voracious. With hair pouffing over his eyes and ears like a 1970s rocker, he was more beauty than brains. I regularly extracted streams of inedibles halfway down his esophagus, which set that little tail stump waggling.

But I failed to notice the fiberglass pillow stuffing he ate while I was on painkillers for a torn hip tendon (the result of that new and untrained Border collie, Olive, pulling at the leash). Two days later I hobbled on crutches into the closest animal ER, at Colorado

State University, which happens to have one of the top two veterinary teaching hospitals in the country. I hesitated for maybe three seconds when the vet gave me the financial estimate for the surgery needed to unblock Houdini's intestines. No, I couldn't let that little dog go yet. Of course I would pay.

At the time of the intestinal surgery the doctors identified a heart murmur and referred him to a veterinary cardiologist. I hadn't even known there was such a specialty. Dr. Bright said the murmur was currently asymptomatic, but we would need to keep a watch on it.

Most of my friends, fellow dog lovers, supported the three-thousand-dollar surgery, but Kelley, who grew up on a farm amid poverty, thought I was nuts. "He's just going to die soon anyway," Kelley said. "Are you going to keep paying for dog surgeries?"

"No," I assured Kelley. "This is it. There are limits."

Are there limits, though? If so, could someone tell me what they are? Is it appropriate to spend vast amounts of money to give our pets a few more years of life, money that could be spent on equally needy humans? To most human beings, it's self-evident that our own species should take priority over others and that interspecies love should respect certain boundaries. But not everyone would agree.

Houdini's decline started with a gag-like cough, so of course I assumed another gastro-intestinal mishap. At that point Houdini was ten years old, which should be adulthood for a dog, but he still chewed compulsively like a puppy, not having grown the brains to discriminate edible from indigestible. I assumed he'd inhaled food down the wrong tube, or aspirated his own vomit. But when the cough didn't go away I took him to my vet. Most dogs hate trips to the clinic, but Houdini loved all the female attention—I should have named him Casanova—and sat on Dr. Plaza's feet waiting to be admired, as he did with all women, and usually succeeded. She pressed her stethoscope to his chest, provoking an erection, a common occurrence for Houdini at a woman's touch. That stethoscope led to more scopes and X-rays and blood draws.

It was a realm I knew too well. Remember, we'd gotten Houdini when Rajiv was being treated for Stage IV colon cancer. Rajiv tried and "failed" chemo drug after chemo drug. When his bilirubin levels soared, indicating severe liver malfunction, doctors told him to consider hospice; it was time to give up and accept his death. "But I want to keep fighting," Rajiv had insisted. We researched clinical trials for chemo study drugs. He even underwent surgery to have a stent inserted in his bile duct to get his bilirubin numbers low enough for a Phase II trial, but still failed to qualify. Because Rajiv was a research scientist in chemical and environmental engineering, and had studied chemotherapy drug production for his PhD, he wanted to be part of a study to at least make his cancer useful to someone else, even when it was clear he wasn't going to survive.

Rajiv was still hoping to get on a new study drug when he went into liver failure. He died on June 2, 2002, three days after turning thirty-eight, leaving me alone to crawl on all fours trying to clean up my dumb cocker's incessant diarrhea before Houdini licked it back up—and then turned to lick the salt off my face.

As he aged, Houdini's heart grew; it swelled with the blood

it couldn't properly pump out. His murmur was so pronounced you could hear it without a stethoscope, or feel it by simply "palpating" with two fingers against his ribcage. By the time Houdini reached eleven years old, already surpassing the life expectancy for a dog in his condition, he was on six pills twice a day—Furosemide (Lasix), Pimobendan, Amlodipine, Benazepril, Spironolactone, and Digoxin—at a collective cost of about $150 a month. I felt guilty paying for them, and guiltier not paying. Many of these drugs are used for the treatment of humans as well. People on Lasix, a diuretic, talk of the particular urgency the drug bestows, sometimes resulting in embarrassing mishaps when a bathroom can't be reached in time. Houdini, long since house-trained, found himself urinating in the middle of the floor, looking as surprised as everyone around him that such a thing was happening. I spread towels around the bathroom, which he sometimes managed to hit. More often, we were back to the early days of my crawling on all fours after his messes.

Throughout all of this, Houdini's amazing, indiscriminate appetite never waned. I took ironic comfort in it.

To each his own, said the lady as she kissed the cow. My father used to deliver that line whenever someone exhibited a clearly unnatural predilection. The line implied that kissing a cow was self-evidently nuts. But these days I can easily imagine myself kissing a Holstein. A near-vegetarian for years now, I no longer find its inherent nuttiness so self-evident. I find myself identifying with those Chick-fil-A cows holding the "Eat Mor Chikin" signs. Then I go on to identify with the chickens. I haven't eaten pork since my childhood reading of *Charlotte's Web* (although, hypocritically, I rarely hesitate to kill spiders).

Were he still alive, my father would think I've crossed over into the unnatural realm. He loved animals, too, and especially dogs, but differently. He didn't believe in keeping them in the house. He came from that earlier generation of pet-owners who would have seen the promotion of pets to family member status as going too far. He might have pointed out that dogs evolved from wolves by following humans and cleaning up their waste; my trailing after Houdini to clean up his waste was completely ass-backwards. Along with my farm-raised friend Kelley, he would have found the whole pet industry—veterinary cardiology, chemotherapy for dogs, canine hydrotherapy centers, doggie day camps—a sign of the complete decadence and imminent fall of American civilization.

Obviously I don't agree. But when I see canine raincoats at PetSmart or an infomercial for Snuggies-for-dogs, even I suspect that we've crossed an invisible line.

All night long Houdini hacked fluid out of his lungs. His rib-shaking coughs burned calories he couldn't afford. Even breathing burned excessive calories. Such labor. His ribs cut into his skin. But if I fed him more to try to fatten him up, he vomited.

He vomited a lot. Yellow splotches, crusting over grass leaves, hid in corners throughout the house. His diarrhea, which he left puddled across my carpet, had a putrid, dead animal stink. I tried to cut all food other than "sensitive systems" kibble out of his diet, and he was a little better at first, but then went back to eating pillow stuffing and pencils and newspapers and chapter one of my new hardcover copy of David Quaamen's *Spillover*, a book about infectious viruses migrating from other animals to humans.

Sometimes I wonder if dogs aren't the most successfully invasive species of all time, more so than rodents, bugs, bacteria, and even viruses. Not only do we host them, not only do we let them eat us out of house and home, not only do we give them our hearts, but we even invent new technologies to extend their scavenging lives.

Part of me told Houdini, "Eat away. Eat yourself dead." I was getting worn out from counting pills, scrubbing carpets, wandering the house sniffing like a dog to locate the sources of urine smells. I was sick of scraping up crystallized yellow crud and washing load after load of rags. Let him eat that damn pillow stuffing; no surgery for him this time.

Most of me was not ready for him to die yet, but part of me was ready to "kevork" him now.

On a Monday morning in June, ten years after Rajiv's death, I brought Houdini, now eleven-and-a-half, back to the cardiologist. He was skin-and-bones by then, using all his calories just to breathe.

The X-rays showed Houdini's heart at twice the size it should be. No fluid in the lungs, but the valve was barely functioning. His heart could burst at any time, and he could "exsanguinate." That was one of four likely death scenarios. I forget the other three. "He's kind of slipped into end stage," the vet said. The X-ray showed Houdini's massive heart pressing all the way against his left-side chest wall. Dr. Bright made a fist to demonstrate. She speculated that his damaged mitral valve only got about twenty percent of the blood through. The other eighty percent "regurgitated." (Appropriately, even his heart was bulimic.)

His coughs, which sounded increasingly boggy, the coughs of a drowning victim pulled at the last minute to land, foretold a grim picture of his likely death route. His lungs would get even wetter, until slowly he drowned in his own blood. Or I could choose to euthanize him at any point. Even now the option "wasn't inappropriate."

Or, Dr. Bright added, almost as an afterthought, though I realized later she was taking care not to be too eager, I could consider one final option. I could have an artificial valve installed.

I immediately thought about the money, and then felt immediately guilty. But thousands of dollars for surgery on a nearly twelve-year-old dog?

"It's a study our chief cardiologist is doing for a new technique to replace a mitral heart valve by catheter, without open-heart surgery. As a Phase I study it can only be performed on end-stage dogs with less than thirty days expected to live. Houdini would be an ideal candidate." Dr. Bright assured me that all costs would be covered by the study. She asked if I knew about clinical trials and what a Phase I study was. I assured her I did. I didn't mention Rajiv.

I met with the cardiac surgeon. This procedure had only been performed once, on Cricket, a Cavalier King Charles spaniel. Cricket didn't make it, but because of other, unrelated complications. Dr. Orton was confident that Houdini was an excellent candidate. I thought of Houdini drowning himself to death. I'd seen the slow, gasping deaths of both Rajiv and my father. I'd rather Houdini died on the table, knowing we'd done everything.

The goal was to perfect the procedure so that it could be transferred for human applications, Dr. Orton told me. "But really I care about the dogs." If Houdini survived the surgery, he'd be the first dog in the world to overcome mitral valve disease without open-heart surgery. It would be a death-defying trick.

Houdini's namesake made a career of defying death. His repertoire of crazy stunts included chaining himself in a locked suitcase underwater. Then at the last minute, magically, he'd escape drowning. But Houdini the dog was no Houdini the magician, I knew. He wasn't special or smart or enduring. He was just a dumb, sweet cocker, who should have died several times over already, filling his guts with pillow stuffing and every chemical and mechanical hazard imaginable.

Every morning up to surgery day, as soon as I awoke I listened for rasping breath and liquid coughs to make sure Houdini hadn't died overnight. Each morning, when I found a spark of the living in him yet, I said, "He's alive! Alive!" My crazed *Bride of Frankenstein* tone set his tail stump waggling.

On the Tuesday morning of surgery day, I settled into the rhythms of the veterinary waiting room, the rhythms of waiting. Yellow-toothed dogs panted in the waiting room. Three-legged dogs hobbled down hallways. Nails clicked on tiles. Rabies tags clinked. Every dog bore shaved patched on a leg or rump or belly. A boxer with a bandaged ear crawled under the vinyl chairs next to me, where his humans sat, and plopped down on the linoleum flooring to cool his belly. He sneezed nervously.

"I'm ready to talk now," a doctor said to a man who'd been sitting in the surgery waiting area since I got there. "Let's go find a room."

"I'm comfortable talking out here," the man said.

"Let's find a room where it might be quieter," the doc answered, ushering the man with a hand gesture toward an open door.

The man's shoulders stiffened. He knew what the room meant.

"That's when you know it's bad," an elderly woman whispered to me as she shifted to my corner. "Good news they give out here, but they don't want you crying in the waiting room. They brought me back to tell me Missy had cancer." Her eyes moistened, but she shook it off. "So now I'm bringing her here every day. I'm an old lady all alone. I have to drive in to Fort Collins from Denver. My hands have arthritis, so it's hard for me to hold the steering wheel for that long. The first day I drove here my car broke down, so I had to buy a new car to take her here. But you do what you have to do, right? So now I'm in even deeper debt. My family says I shouldn't hold on to my dog like I do and spend all my money on her. You need to let her go, they tell me. But where are they when they're not giving advice? Missy is all I've got."

I remembered that waiting room from thirteen years ago, when Rajiv staggered out of the GI lab after his first sigmoidoscopy, shaking his head. The gastroenterologist came out behind him. That time they didn't take me back for the bad news. Dr. Compton had held a glossy photo, all pinks and reds. I didn't know what I was seeing at the time; he could have told me it was a heart and I, unable to tell the organ from a tumor, would have believed him. The doctor looked to me for confirmation that I understand, though, and because I was unable to speak, I nodded.

I nodded to Missy's human now. You do what you have to do.

Since then, I've known waiting rooms. From Rajiv's chemo, radiation, and surgical procedures, I thought I'd learned the art of waiting—how to pace myself, how to ward off both hopes and fears. Hope is the bigger danger. If you must what-if, better to rehearse the worst-case scenario.

So I inventoried all the changes I could make after Houdini died. I could put out throw pillows on the sofa. I could leave pens and pencils astray on the table, or even the floor. I could get the carpets cleaned and stop smelling urine. I could put toilet paper rolls back in their cubbies. I wasn't like Missy's poor owner. I could live without Houdini.

But even as I thought this I began to feel twinges in my own heart. Probably just the usual chest wall muscle spasms I got from time to time. But what if I had a heart attack in the middle of Houdini's surgery? How embarrassing would that be? And would they take me back and treat me with all the other large animals? Or maybe I counted as a small animal. Would they lay me out in the same OR and repair my heart alongside Houdini's?

"They're closing," my human liaison, Gail, popped out to report. "Give me five." She squeezed my hand and winked. I did a big dog-sigh, the kind they emit after circling three times in bed. "Now he's headed to post-op, where the critical period begins."

Oh. I thought the critical period had just ended.

I tried not to imagine a pain down my left arm.

Next Dr. Orton came out in his scrubs. Everything looked good. But don't ride too high on the roller coaster. Cricket, too, had looked good at this point. Still, Houdini's heart was already smaller, Dr. Orton said. As soon as they inserted the new valve, "his heart gave a big sigh."

Dr. Orton mentioned, before returning to the CCU, that Houdini was given a pig's valve. This nagged at the edges of my consciousness as I waited. Wasn't the pig already using that valve? Is a dog's life worth more than a pig's? I guess I'd assumed the new heart valve was artificial, part of the contraption. I'm glad I didn't know before that the heart valve came from a pig. I would have had to go on record as choosing my Houdini's life over a pig's, with no good justification, rational or otherwise. Ladies who kiss cows also kiss pigs, fellow mammals who exhibit an intelligence, emotional life, and appetite not unlike Houdini's.

Beside me a pug began snorting so violently he nearly choked himself.

I waited.

And then Gail reported a "hiccup." She put her hand on my knee. "Houdini's bleeding a little."

"Okay," I said.

"They're giving him transfusions."

"Okay."

"But he's calm. Everybody's calm."

"Okay."

Gail explained how they were trying to balance his numbers to keep him smack between clotting and bleeding out. It was tricky. She squeezed my knee before leaving for more news.

This was the point when Cricket bled out.

A dead dog was wheeled out on a cart. Blankets covered most of the body but a big, pink, lab-like snout stuck out, as if allowing the dead dog to breathe. The human following behind the cart kept her head down. The boxer-owning woman next to me burst into tears.

Dr. Orton returned to say that the bleeding seemed to have stopped. Behind him a young man in scrubs wheeled the empty cart back, the blankets limp.

Finally they took me back to see Houdini. No, the bleeding hadn't stopped, but they were "keeping up with it." And there he was, his head on a pillow, his tongue hanging out to the side, a yellow tube running through his right nostril. I could see his heart beating against his shaved chest, slower and calmer than it had been in two years. Did he recognize me through those groggy eyes and that snoring nose? Hard to tell.

On the way out I said to Dr. Orton, "Even if Houdini doesn't pull through, that's still a big step forward for your study, isn't it?"

"That's not good enough," he said. "We're going for complete recovery."

I found out later that Houdini was being tended to by a team of twelve cardiologists and five anesthesiologists. That doesn't even count the ICU team. Gail said a greyhound donated fresh blood that morning in case Houdini needed it. Not just any greyhound, either, but the greyhound belonging to one of the top veterinary anesthesiologists in the country, who was part of Houdini's team.

All this for Houdini, my dumb little dog.

The truth is that I would have donated my own blood if it worked across species. I suspect that every human in this waiting room would gladly bleed for our dogs. We wouldn't just give our life-savings for our dogs; we'd give our very life-blood as well.

The next morning Houdini stepped forward and butted my chest with his head to induce me to rub his ears. He recognized me. I offered him small finger-scoops of low residue wet food, and he nearly snapped my fingers off as he chomped. He was back.

Maybe.

Then the waiting game really started. Dr. Ames, taking over for Dr. Orton and Dr. Bright, regularly updated me. Houdini survived the surgery, but the bleeding problem persisted. Then he stopped bleeding and almost immediately formed a clot on his new valve, which itself was working beautifully. They watched and waited and measured and watched and waited and measured for two days. The clot grew. On Friday morning they decided to blast him with a clot-buster. The clot disappeared but he started bleeding again, not only at every incision site but internally, in his chest cavity, making it hard to fill his lungs.

The next time I went back to the Critical Care Unit I saw a different dog from my happy Houds. He lifted his head to greet me but couldn't manage more. For the first time he didn't get up on his feet at my arrival, didn't butt me for a petting or look for food. His eyes told me he was spent. He'd been a good sport through the surgery, the injections, the transfusions, the tubes, and the electrodes, but now he'd had about enough. He was ready to go.

Or maybe that was complete projection. I was getting tired. I'd been through the long succession of bad news before. I was ready for closure. But maybe Houdini wasn't. Maybe he was just a dumb dog whose body wanted to live and whose mind/will/spirit didn't know what the fuck was going on.

On Sunday Dr. Ames explained how when they bust a clot it goes somewhere else in the body before dissolving. It might go somewhere harmless, or it might go to the kidney or lungs or brain. "Fortunately with dogs we can get away with a small amount of brain loss," she smiled. "It's not like he's going to be teaching English literature. He just needs to snuggle and be sweet."

"But he had so few brains to start with!" I said, beginning to hope that he'd survive to be an even dumber dog than he already was.

By Monday morning he looked better. He stood for me, and

even ate a few pellets of kibble out of my hand. His hot tongue licked my palm for crumbs.

But in the afternoon "he had bleeding." They "tapped" his chest and transfused blood. No sign of clotting, the even worse danger, but the bleeding was "worrisome."

When I walked in the CCU he tried to look at me through his third eyelid. Slowly his eyes cleared and he even tried to stand for me but immediately toppled. He wouldn't take food from my hand. When Houdini stops eating, I thought . . .

Dr. Ames expected him to make it through the night. "He's a fighter," she said. This ridiculous dog had really redeemed himself in the end, as if he found his calling after all. Christians have a concept, I'm told, about how God asks you to serve not in spite of your deficiencies but through them. Houdini's faults made him a great research dog. His eating disorder, compelling him to eat through illness, his sluggishness and slacker nature, his appetite for love, his dumb trust and forgiveness, even the deafness of his latter geriatric years, which shielded him from CCU beeps and barks, all made him an excellent patient, and a well-loved one. I made fun of him all his life, but in the end he served us nobly.

I said goodbye. I also said, "Keep fighting." Even as I was saying the words, Houdini's eyeballs were rolling back, his eyelashes fluttering. His little front paw twitched, and twitched again. "Oh look," Dr. Ames smiled, "he's dreaming."

"I hope it's a good dream," I said. "I hope he's eating everything he's ever wanted to."

"Yes." She caught the somberness of my tone and matched it. "We all do."

❧

I knew as soon as I heard Dr. Wells' recorded phone call the next day. She said they were "all very concerned about Houdini" and that I should "come right down" as soon as I got the message. Earlier in the day I'd had a good morning with him. Dr. Wells had brought Houdini outside into the sun, and we sat out in the grass, Houdi's chin resting on my knee. When we got back inside he gulped water and ate food from my hand. Maybe his name really would prove prescient and he'd cheat death once more.

But when they walked me back to the CCU that Tuesday afternoon, I wondered how bad it would look if I didn't cry. I didn't want to cry. I didn't need to cry.

Houdini—"the Houds"—lifted his eyes to me but nothing more. Someone had spread his floppy ears out like Dumbo in flight. "Is that blood on his nose?" I asked.

Dr. Ames touched her finger to the red spot. "No, it's lipstick," she said. "From one of us kissing him."

Then I realized that the line of women behind me, his team of doctors and techs and vet students, all were crying. They passed the box of Kleenex around.

I shouldn't have worried about not crying enough. Now I worried I was crying too much. I could barely get my throat to choke out the words "I'm ready."

Dr. Ames stepped forward with the needle.

In the end, Houdini did not eat himself to death, and maybe he does live up to his name after all. Not only has he been immortalized in literary and veterinary publications, but the data generated by his surgery and autopsy have already led to improvements on the valve apparatus that should make it successful in the future. Or at least that's what Dr. Ames told me, and I don't think she was just trying to be nice.

My father had mitral valve disease and died of a (possibly related) stroke. Heart trouble runs in my family, both sides. Maybe by the time I need a mitral valve replacement I'll receive the Houdini-Orton technique. That's the ending this narrative demands—the narrative of dog, as man's best friend, serving and saving the human. The other story of human serving dog—of pouring all this money and time and energy and expertise into "just a dog"—seems less satisfying, less justifiable.

Or does it?

Dr. Orton had said he really cared about the dogs as much as the humans, and it made me happy to hear him say this. But I sometimes wonder if Kelley and my father are right: we're all nuts. Cousins of that cow-kissing lady, we devote our lives to predatory scavengers. People say our dogs' love for us is unconditional, but sometimes it's our love for the dogs that's unconditional. We're all part of an experiment in cross-species heart surgery.

That morning in the CSU veterinary teaching hospital when I learned that Houdini was end-stage, I cupped my palm against the left side of Houdi's chest. His heart beat so palpably, so laboriously. It felt as if I held it in my hand.

8

Rescue Dogs

A rescue dog story is supposed to end in rescue. It would go like this: slowly and incrementally, my rescue dog and I would heal together. We would follow complementary, interweaving narratives, with my Border collie's story circling and herding mine. We would end up rescuing each other just as the narrative gate closes. That's the way dog stories are supposed to go: the dog ends up rescuing the human as much as the human rescues the dog. Certainly I needed rescuing. But stories can sometimes stray off-track.

Humans are creatures of narrative. Some scholars even say that the need for narrative, for a storyline, is as hard-wired into the human make-up as the herding instinct is in Border collies or the prey drive in wolves. Even disciplines far afield from literature—like, say, psychotherapy—compose stories that progress, climax, and resolve. I got a taste of this in grief therapy. The grief narrative (or "grief journey," as the therapist called it) is supposed to follow a hero's journey down into the underworld and back up again, traveling through stages of "grief work" like Odysseus through treacherous seas. Finally, after climax and resolution, in which the grieved "comes to terms with loss," integrating it into her new reality, she "moves on." During this latter phase, says Therese Rando, a major figure in Grief Studies, the griever must move through the following "Six R Processes of Mourning": "Recognize the Loss"; "React to the Separation"; "Recollect and Reexperience the Deceased and the Relationship"; "Relinquish the Old Attachments to the Deceased and the Old Assumptive World"; "Readjust to Move Adaptively into the New World Without Forgetting the Old"; and "Reinvest" in new attachments.

I did three of my "Six R Processes of Mourning," but I got stuck on relinquishing, readjusting, and reinvesting. Moving adaptively has never been my forte, even under the best of circumstances, which these were not. I didn't want to move on; I just wanted Rajiv back. I wanted to resume my "happily ever after" storyline, the one where we grew old together and held hands on our way into urology appointments.

Failure to complete this journey indicates, to therapists, "complicated grief"—grief gone wrong—which calls for intervention. "Complicated" in the medical sense means not so much intricate as winding, tortuous, obstructed, never-ending. It includes *delayed* grieving, *absent* grieving, *acute* or *exaggerated* grieving, and *unresolved* or *chronic* grieving. A grief journey demands resolution. Complicated grievers live in endless, unresolved stories: the Odysseuses never heard from again, the Penelopes still weaving. We are the sheep who wouldn't be herded into the pen. We fail to close our narrative gates.

At first people put on their sad faces to talk to me, but in American culture the acceptable grieving period is about two months, and so they soon began nudging me to "move on" and start dating again. Idling in grief, I'd become a bad mourner, endlessly weaving and unweaving my story in journals and essays, sabotaging closure.

I briefly tried an online dating service anyway, but found myself gazing longingly at the photos not of the men but of their dogs. I nearly responded to one ad purely for the Malamute puppy cradled in the suitor's arms.

I suppose that when I adopted Olive I was trying to write myself into a rescue narrative, the kind with healing and closure. Maybe this was an attempt to "reinvest" in new attachments, one of the R Processes I still needed to complete. It wasn't conscious when I made that fateful trip to the Humane Society, but the pull of narratives works at the unconscious level even more powerfully than at the conscious level. I suspect that I was already groping for a story-line when I found myself looking at the dogs awaiting adoption and that two-year-old Border collie cast her spell. "Olive" was entirely black except for her paws, her belly, and the white racing stripe that ran from her skullcap to her nose. As I fingered the dog's velvet black ears through the cage door, the intake clerk told me that "Olive" had been removed by Animal Control from a dog hoarder, an old woman who kept her eight dogs tied to trees all day long. "You can't do that to any dog, much less a Border collie," the intake clerk said. Border collies are the smartest and most energetic of dogs, and also the most neurotic. If they're not given a job, they go crazy.

Confined by a hoarder: my rescue fantasies awoke. Like grief, dog rescue is a genre, with its own pre-scribed story. Already I was plotting recovery and resurrection.

I've already written about what happened next: Olive's anxieties and neuroses, her fervent energy, her aggression, her terrorizing my other dogs, my many attempts to tame her, my despair. In the dog park and on walks, she became territorial and "resource protective," meaning she guarded her food source. That would be me. If I stood still, she circled around me, defining our space, and then launched an aggressive herding nip at any dog who tried to enter the three-foot bubble for a petting. Olive preferred Hindu warrior-goddess mythology over my compact rescue narrative.

In some versions of that pre-scripted rescue narrative, the owner, through training her dog, learns important lessons about human behavior. But Olive's issues only resembled human ones in the most general of ways. She experiences a very different world than primates do. I knew from my other dogs about the primacy of smell, but not of space. Now I'm hypersensitive to it. Olive's world is all about invisible boundaries. We move through constantly shifting precincts, across sentried borders, into disputed territories. The zone at the gate. The zone around the water bowl. The zone around me or anyone carrying treats (the T-word, not to be spoken aloud). These spaces, constantly violated, need constant patrolling.

Many of Olive's issues, especially her hyper-awareness of space, come from her being a Border collie, a breed made for herding sheep by impinging on their safety zones. As I've written before, I read extensively about the breed in hopes of translating her neuroses. Border collies need a finely tuned sense of space to know just how much pressure, and at just what distance, to put on a sheep's invisible space bubble. This hard-wired herding instinct was developed centuries ago, in the hilly borderlands between England and Scotland, when Roman herders interbred their pastoral dogs with the local rock-dwellers, and then modified the prey drive to stop before killing. These borderland collies stalk their woolly prey with intensity and precision, but never catch. A herding dog's chase drive is as strong as ever, but, stunted, it never achieves closure. The closest it gets is to lead sheep to enclosure.

The herding impulse inspires awe. Even if it's a human-created instinct—an artificial redirection of the prey drive—it feels no less primal. Border collies' drive to herd involves not so much pleasure (as the lust of the hunt might) as compulsion. Typical of her breed, Olive doesn't play with other dogs. In fact, she doesn't "play" at all. Border collies are known as the workaholics of the dog world. If they can't work, they're miserable. They'll create work for themselves, even if it takes the form of self-destruction. At least that's a purpose.

I can understand that impulse. The year of Rajiv's cancer, I'd channeled all my energy into his care. Oddly, the worst year of my life was the most fulfilling. I knew what I had to do. Rajiv wanted to go down fighting, so daily, doggedly, I fought with receptionists to squeeze us in earlier appointment slots, and with doctors to put Rajiv on trial drugs. I drove Rajiv to appointments, sat with him during chemo infusions, filled prescriptions, argued with insurance, slept overnight on hospital chairs. I had purpose. It was afterward, with nothing to be done, that crazed me.

In zoos, animals with too little stimulation can develop "stereotypies"—repetitive and often self-destructive behaviors, similar to the "perseveration" of autistic children. We see head-bobbing bears, bulimic gorillas, and lions pacing their cages long after the concrete has rubbed their paws raw. Domestic dogs are notorious for stereotypies, even when their cage is a whole house or yard or even park: the Lab who licks his paw ragged, the Brittany spaniel who chases shadows. Border collies perseverate especially severely. Olive runs in circles around the park, or, more commonly, fence-runs. Back and forth she goes along the border, fueled by some urgent force of nature. Any dog who tries to interfere with her work faces Medusan fury. In the summer she plows a dirt path into the grass. In the winter snow she dredges canals along the fence, leaving tell-tale, "Olive-was-here" lines. She monitors squirrels as if they were sheep, making wide out-runs and then narrowing her circles, but if she gets any enjoyment from herding squirrels, it's a desperate kind of joy.

Funktionslust refers to the pleasure animals take in doing what they were bred to do. It's as if Olive's body-mind keeps seeking her function, but can never find it, much less achieve it. She roams the dog park—and the world—as if in search of a way to express drives she doesn't understand. Constantly frustrated, she never finds her purpose.

Meanwhile, I took Olive to multiple obedience classes, which train the owner more than the dog. While I was a C student, Olive was brilliant, and quickly picked up the basics of sit, down, stay, and come, along with tricks like handshake, high five, double-five, high five from behind, rollover, play dead, shimmy, do the can-can, weave figure-eights, back-up-like-a-truck, and "say your prayers." Together we mastered heel, advanced stays, and some basic agility course skills. But she failed the basic Canine Good Citizen test because the instant I gave Olive a release signal ("All done"), she preemptively snarled at a Chihuahua in the vicinity of her treats. She made puppies cry and grown dogs whimper. Other classmates kept their distance, and even the various trainers gave up on Olive and advised that I never place her in situations where both treats and other dogs co-exist. Thus ended the agility classes.

One trainer, who specialized in "reactive" dogs, taught me to walk away from Olive when she protected me, so as to frustrate, rather than reward, her actions. It takes real discipline and trust to walk away from your dog when she's about to lunge at another. I had to retrain my instincts. Since Olive was always protective, I learned to keep walking in the dog park, around and around the perimeter, so as to never let her claim a space. If I stood a minute to chat with another human, Olive might nip at their dog, and I'd have to leave abruptly. So as Olive developed her repetitive behaviors, I mirrored her, walking in circles around the dog park or back and forth along the fence. The progress narrative spiraled back into itself.

I looked into sheep-herding, and we drove out to a windswept, face-chapping ranch where real Border collies and their handlers delivered sheep into pens. I'd hoped that Olive would see the sheep and, in just one look, would understand who she was. She'd smell the musty wool and hear the call of her shepherd ancestors from the British borderlands. She would know her destiny. We would transform into one of the middle-aged women and their Border collies who, in the fields all around us, worked as teams, expertly herding sheep to their pens in smooth lines and arcs. I'd decided that if Olive took to herding like it was her calling, I'd invest my time and money into this new sport that was already freezing me to the bones.

The trainer started Olive with goats. Olive took a few runs at them and then became fascinated with the scattered pellets of goat poop, which she grazed on for the rest of the (rather expensive) session. The trainer shouted over the wind that if I were determined to train Olive to herd I'd probably succeed. But she didn't act as if she'd discovered what was missing all her life. It was too late. Olive was already three years old, a young adult. Herding is like language acquisition in humans; the capacity may be hard-wired, but after a critical age the language will never be native. No matter how proficient the speaker becomes, the language remains foreign.

When we got home, Olive darted into the back yard and looked through her peephole in the fence. She'd been communing with the autistic girl next door. Sometimes they called to each other in yips and eeps that trebled into shrieks. I don't know if they were enjoying or tormenting each other. I don't know if either of them knew. They seemed to be obeying a call deeper than joy, more urgent than pain.

When the autistic girl moved away a few months later, Olive perseverated at the fence for weeks, alternately pacing and searching through the peephole for what was missing.

Over time, I did, of course, bond with Olive, and came to love her fiercely, even on the days I hated her. Slowly she loosened up a notch or two, and assumed the role of protector, rather than assailant, of my other dogs. The day she nipped a boisterously humping pit bull off old Pretzel's back and then took on the pit's wrathful jaw, she became a full family member. Her white belly got extra rubs that night. She went from being a miserable thing to a creature a little less miserable. It was, at best, a stunted rescue narrative.

Then, in quick succession, my three older dogs died. Each new grief compounded the primal grief, the one I never "got over" but kept circling back to. Much as I tried to find inner strength and resilience, I just couldn't heal. I've come to accept that I may never heal. I may always be stuck wandering halfway between the underworld and the living one aboveground. Olive, too, may always remain damaged goods: my albatross, my nemesis, my partner.

Olive ends up being the one I grow old with. At eleven years old now, her urology issues have begun. I recognize in her gait the beginnings of an arthritic limp because I've had the same one, and tried to hide it in the same ways, before my bilateral hip joint replacement surgeries. Even bêtes noire grow old.

Recently I've started calling her "Sweetheart" in spite of all evidence, and, when I pet her as if she were a sweet dog, she softens under my palm, then throws herself onto her back to offer me her blue-scarred belly. When I rub it, she grunts like the old woman she now is.

I've concluded, too late, that Border collies cannot be pets. They are forces of nature. Confining a Border collie in a house is like tying one to a tree—different in degree, but similar in emotional damage. Olive remains stuck as a pet. For her, it's too late to become a herder or a farm dog or an agility dog. A dog with a job and a purpose. Olive's story will not resolve. Her tracks, like mine, mark out circles and spirals, dashes and zig-zags. She follows an obsessive-compulsive narrative, stuck in repetitive loops, moving from trick to trick, from food bowl to food bowl, from hoarder to hoarder. We don't all get to achieve *funktionslust*. Sometimes just functioning is the achievement. Olive will persist in expressing a herding instinct that she doesn't understand, and whose fulfillment will ever elude her. She'll keep searching, without ever knowing it, for that wayward sheep to set right. The rescue narrative remains an elusive fairy tale.

The "grief journey" narrative, too, may be an imposed fairy tale, from which I've irrevocably strayed. In life, if not in literature, narrative structures often fail, much as we try to resurrect them again and again. We live in geometries far more complicated than the narrative arc. Not everyone gets saved. Not every wayward sheep gets herded back into its pen.

Let it stray.

9

Secondhand Happiness

I've never gotten happiness. It is to me what insulin is to a diabetic: I can't manufacture my own. At best, I dose myself with infusions from other donors, human and otherwise. Even when I receive a bolus, though, I still don't "get" happiness. I fundamentally cannot understand it.

Widowhood deserves some of the blame for my disability, but even before my life partner died and I went underground, I never did realize happiness. Back when the love of my life still lived, though, I could at least borrow hits off his abundant stash. Post-loss, happiness eluded me more than ever.

Religious teachings, self-help gurus, and conventional grief counselors offered wise guidance. Live in the moment, they all said, and be present. Try meditating. Immerse yourself in nature. Say thank you to the universe. I tried, but the present was always somewhere else. Maybe happiness is not so much a substance like insulin as an instinct. Perhaps the capacity for joy is as an extra-sensory sense but, lacking it, I'm confined to just the basic five. Functionally humor-deaf and happiness-blind, I turn to guide dogs, the closest to nature I can get. "Because dogs," is what I keep reminding myself whenever I'm feeling a touch suicidal and looking for a reason to live. Dogs transmit secondhand happiness to me.

Some people object that ascribing happiness to dogs is anthropomorphism, a mere projection of human emotions onto nonhuman animals. We can't assume other species experience emotions in the same ways that we do; their experience of the world, and of themselves (to the extent that they have "selves") must be radically different from ours. For now, I'm willing to risk anthropomorphizing dogs, because if I can't interpret much of canine behavior as happiness then I'll never find it.

My first stab at adopting a dog on my own after my life partner died, however, went awry. Olive, a black Border collie with a white bib and booties who hexed me with her stare at the rescue shelter, was supposed to be my salvation. Instead, she was a bigger mess than I was; more depressed, more anxious, more obsessive-compulsive, more all-around neurotic. She'd gotten a rough start in life, having ended up at the shelter after being rescued from a hoarder who'd tied her to a tree. That's enough to mess up any dog, but more so a high-strung, already territorial Border collie. It gave Olive canine OCD, and she engaged in "perseverating" behaviors such as fence-running and incessant barking. Her tail rarely wagged; it mostly drooped, unless she was shrieking at a squirrel, when it stiffened.

Dogs were supposed to instinctively get the be-here-now thing, to radiate what we anthropomorphically call happiness. Not my little bitch. I came to think of her as my bête noire, the embodiment of my own psychic mess of anxiety and depression. Winston Churchill referred to his depression metaphorically as a black dog; mine was made flesh.

Like depression, Olive cried out for constant attention, along with guidance and exercise. After hours and hours of obedience training classes, we managed to make a bit of progress. I learned to assert the confidence, clarity, and certainty I certainly didn't feel, and she learned to sit, stay, come, heel, and perform silly tricks. Army crawl. Say your prayers. Play dead.

Gradually, Olive transformed from a miserable thing to a less miserable thing, from pathologically anxious to merely neurotic. That achievement gave me a kind of fulfillment, but although fulfillment may run deeper than happiness, it's not as present. Olive, too, achieved moments of fulfillment as, purpose-driven, she perfectly executed the jobs I gave her to do. But I could not teach her how to be happy. I couldn't even teach her how to play, either with me or with other dogs. She didn't have the happiness instinct either. She could master tricks faster than I could invent them, but couldn't get play.

Instead, at the dog park, she sniffed for spots to re-mark and protected her food resource (me), but saved the bulk of her energy for border patrol, guarding the fence from outside invaders such as bicyclists, other dogs, and—the horror—horses. She seemed to enjoy, in her dog way, nosing and assessing all manner of putrescent refuse on our walks, but it was a workaholic's twisted version of joy.

While Olive's anxiety abated over time, that only enhanced her loneliness and depression. So I tried adopting another dog for her. Tiger, an untrained, energetic, ridiculously playful husky-terrier mix, looked up at me from his rescue shelter cage, framing each amber eye in a metal-wire square. The rescue group said he'd been found wandering a six-lane highway in Texas. When they brought him from the high kill shelter there up to Colorado, they named him Tigger after Winnie the Pooh's friend, and he showed that same artless exuberance as the fictional foil to Eeyore. (They changed his name to Tiger when they realized how "Tigger" might be misheard when yelled across a field.)

Sir Scruffulous, I called him. He looked like a cartoon husky, or like a Disney version of a wolf, all bristly with grandpa eyebrows and whiskers. Unfortunately, El Tigré turned out to be a wild thing. On our first trip to the dog park in the winter, he pulled mittens off people's hands and ran, proudly, with his new toys. Three separate times he bounded over the fence and off into the woods.

So now I had two neurotic dogs.

But Tiger had the happiness instinct that Olive and I lacked. With training, he became tamer. Still, he generated so much energy that he forced Olive to play. She snarled, but he wouldn't take no for an answer, bounding up to her and giving her first a play-bow and then a husky body-slam. Olive nipped at his limbs, herding-style. He flattened his front legs again, gave a "woof," and then grabbed her scruff and shook. She flipped under him with some spontaneous canine jiu-jitsu move and grabbed his scruff. Her tail began to wag, and not in that stiff, pre-fight way. Tiger shook free. With a clump of her fellow hellhound's white fur snagged in her teeth, Olive play-bowed for more. I'd never seen her play-bow before and didn't think she could be taught to do so, any more than my depression itself could be taught to play-bow, so at first I thought she was stretching. But no. Tiger gladly accepted her play-bow, and they scrapped once again, Olive's whole butt wagging along with her tail. Tiger had taught my bête noire to play.

Maybe happiness could be learned, after all.

Now, a bit tamer, Tiger makes me laugh out loud at least once every day. His husky mask mimics a raised-eyebrow look of eternal surprise over his terrier-whiskered muzzle. He's mastered the "I'm

innocent, and I'm sorry, and I didn't do it, and I'll never do it again"
look that's now been officially declared an evolutionary advantage.
Tiger's thick-bristled tail and upright ears, outlined in black like
a cartoon drawing, make at least twenty different expressions,
mixing mischief with curiosity and anticipation with present joy.

One day, as I lay fetal-positioned in bed with an advancing mi-
graine, Tiger crashed into bed with me and circled three times
before rounding his butt into my belly, making a yang for my yin.
Olive, now an aging diva, grunt-plopped onto the foot of the bed.

Still trying to crack the happiness code, I'd recently read that
happiness should not even be the goal. The real goal is to shift your
emotional set-point to enable moments of unprompted happiness
to happen. Happiness, I'd read, is that fleeting feeling that all's
right with the world, or at least that the world is as it should be.

I try to imagine that feeling. Most mornings I feel almost the
opposite: that something is terribly wrong, but I'm not sure what.
I could list a thousand things that are wrong, both with the world
and with myself, and I often do. When your thirty-seven-year-
old life partner goes into the sigmoidoscopy with hemorrhoids
and comes out with terminal colon cancer, it's hard to trust the
universe. But if I'm honest I know that none of the thousand-and-
one wrongs I list, not even the big one, is the true source of my
unhappiness; they're just convenient alibis. So I try to imagine the
opposite of feeling all's-wrong-with-the-world.

Instead, a spontaneous grunt as ample as Olive's loosens out of
me. As if voice-activated, Tiger uncurls to stamp my cheek with
his pink-and-black-mottled nose, and then to sniff at my cheek, my
neck, my ear. His tail thumps before he drops his head back onto
front paws. I feel oddly compelled to mimic him. I sniff at his cheek.

I can't say it smells good—a bale of hay sprinkled with Parmesan cheese and a dusting of coriander—but, I realize, I recognize this smell. It's Tiger's smell. It's Tiger's smell! And I recognize it! I dig my nose in deeper, savoring this slightly fermented, slightly starchy flavor, this mouth-feel in the nose. Is this how dogs feel when they sniff? Each smell is its own kind of now.

Maybe, instead of anthropomorphizing dogs, the trick is to canine-ize yourself.

Olive wanders over, her black nose twitching, assessing, as she sniffs my ear. Now thirteen-years-old and recently diagnosed with a heart murmur, she might not be long for this world. Her black face shows white eyebrows and a white "Got Milk?" mustache at the corners of her jaw. She jumps into bed with an *oof*. "It's hard, isn't it, being an aging diva?" I say to her. I burrow my nose into my bête noire's scruff. Charcoal dusted with cocoa powder. Again, it's a smell I recognize, a smell I didn't even know I knew. It isn't a good smell or a bad smell. It's just a smell. Olive's smell. Undertones of cardamom from deep, deep down. I fill my nostrils with it, and try to hold the scent inside them even as I breathe out through my mouth. For just this half-moment, which I know will pass, is already passing, I can almost feel, just beneath my sacrum, the twinges of a vestigial tail trying to wag.

10

The Spot

Rajiv died in the middle of the living room on the bed that hospice set up to prevent bedsores. I've been telling this story over and over, these many times, revisiting the same spot. That's how grief works. That's how memory works.

After Rajiv stopped breathing and his face relaxed into a death mask, Pretzel jumped off the bed and huddled under the futon, where he stayed while the funeral home took away Rajiv's body, and stayed for the next few weeks, coming out only to eat and vomit and pee.

Although house-trained for years, and although he still peed out in the backyard too, Pretzel started peeing in the middle of the living room. Right on the spot where Rajiv died. Which I cleaned up, crying, all the more pained because it was in the sacred spot. And then I made the connection. Pretzel was marking the spot.

I've told this story before. I will tell it again. The spot remains, whatever bacterial or fungal cultures it harbors burgeoning underneath the repeatedly wiped surface.

It was a stain I could never remove. No matter how thoroughly I cleaned up the urine, and no matter what fancy urine-removing liquids I bought, Pretzel and then my other two dogs continued peeing in the same spot. For years. Even after I pulled up the carpet, deep-treated the floorboards with KILZ, and put down laminate flooring, Pretzel kept peeing there.

Even after Pretzel and the other two dogs died, a new set of dogs maintained the spot. These new dogs don't even know about Rajiv (though surely they've smelled traces of him in the house, even still). But they know that this is a meaningful spot. Meaningful to them, perhaps, only because they can smell the trace of urine deep, deep down, and need to maintain it, to top it. It's a shrine that they maintain in our living room, a living shrine, made in the medium specific to canine communication.

This is a spot where cultures meet, in many senses of the word culture. Along with the bacterial cultures down under the floorboards, there's also the culture of dogs here, leaving messages across time to future dogs to recognize this spot as a place of meaning. I have no idea what the spot means to Olive and Tiger, but I do know it's a meaningful place.

I return to this spot, telling over and over these stories of dogs and death, searching for new meanings, covering and recovering my words, alert for new messages. I tell them to others I don't know, in the hopes that when you read it, you, too, will sense meaning, and, perhaps, respond.

BIOGRAPHICAL NOTE

Deborah Thompson is a professor of English at Colorado State University, where she teaches literature and creative nonfiction. She has published creative and critical essays, and has won the *Missouri Review* and *Iowa Review* awards in creative nonfiction, as well as a Pushcart Prize. She lives with her dogs in Fort Collins, Colorado.